A GEORGIA SOLDIER

SOLDIER

IN THE CIVIL WAR

1861-1865

BY ROBERT D. CHAPMAN

PUBLISHER'S NOTES

Robert Chapman's memoir of his service in the Confederate Army is full of excitement and daring. Much of the account below relates his capture by Federal troops and imprisonment. He nearly died of illness before escaping and the most interesting part of his memoir is about his long journey to return to Confederate lines, where he resumed duty.

Robert Duncan Chapman was born on December 8th, 1839 in Georgia to William Hilliard Judson Chapman and Temperance Honor Chapman, the third of their seven children and five half-siblings. In 1867, Chapman married Eugenia Alice McNeil, with whom he had four children. Living in Cotton Hill, Georgia, Chapman worked as a dry goods merchant. The family moved to Texas and by 1880, Chapman listed his occupation as "ice cream dealer." He appears to have continued in retail work for the bulk of his working life. Eugenia died in 1906 and by 1920, eighty year old Robert was living with a daughter and her family, and working at the courthouse in Houston as a bailiff, a position he still held at 89!

Chapman held an honorary title of Commander in Chief of the Confederate Veterans association, a role he cherished enough to have engraved on his tombstone. He died on August 7, 1934 and is buried in Nacogdoche, Texas.

A CONFEDERATE SOLDIER IN THE CIVIL WAR

The bombardment of Fort Sumter in Charleston harbor summoned every loyal patriot to the defense of his section, and on the 1st of August, 1861, I enlisted in the service at Colquitt, Miller County, Ga., and participated in the hasty organization of a company of 112 men known as the Miller County Wild Cats, and went into camp on Huckle Berry Ridge, near Wild Cat Creek in a remote section of southwest Georgia, known as the wiregrass section of the state. Cattle, cow hides, peas, pork, possum and potatoes were legal tender; fish, game and gophers were plentiful round about the camp; some of the company were fishermen, some hunters, and the balance were fiddlers and gopher-diggers, so that we had wild meats most of the time, gopher soup some of the time, and music in camp all of the time. Our captain, B. R. Kendrick tendered our services to the confederate authorities, but the answer came back that they could not arm and equip us for immediate service. The company was very much disappointed at this indefinite delay and applied to the Governor of Georgia for marching orders.

The Governor promptly accepted our services and directed us to arm our company the best we could and report to the camp of instruction, near Savannah, Georgia.

Accordingly the company armed itself with every death-dealing instrument that could be procured, each man had a bowie knife, dirk or dagger, leather belt and scabbard, securely belted around his body, and the old rifle and shot gun, long used in the chase by the old citizens and for home protection were taken down from the rack above the cottage door. Both this, the companion of his youthful sport, and the affectionate son of his old age were contributed as a sacrificial offering upon the altar of his country. Just before leaving camp, a very amusing incident occurred which changed the sadness of the hour into laughter, when an old pioneer hunter—wearing a coon-skin cap and leather breeches—came rushing in with an old, single barrel shot gun and said to his son, "I don't want any war in mine, but if you will go, here's old Betsy; take her and give the Yankees hell." Thus equipped, and well loaded with good things from home to eat on the way, we started on the war path.

After several day's march we arrived at the camp of instruction where we met nine other companies from different portions of the state and proceeded to organize the 1st Regiment of Georgia Volunteers and were mustered into state service for a term of six months, and the Miller County Wild Cats became Company E, the Banner company in the 1st Georgia State Troops and I was promoted from a private to the rank of Sergeant Major of the Regiment, which position I very much appreciated. We reported to General Harrison of Savannah for duty and we were ordered to encamp near about Savannah for coast defense. We commenced fortifying the city against the approach of the Federal fleet; Fort Boggs and other fortifications were hastily constructed for the protection of the city from the approach of the enemy by land. This work was principally done by the soldiers of the 1st Georgia Regiment; five companies constituted a fatigue detail, while the other five companies of the Regiment constituted a school of instruction in military tactics. This fatigue service and camp duties were considered a very great hardship; we had left our homes and fields of labor behind us and now thrilled with martial music and military activities, we had caught a vision of the palms of victory and crowns of glory won upon the battle field. We were very anxious to go to the front fearing the war would close before our six months of service in Georgia would expire, and we would not be permitted to share the honors in store for our victorious armies. These visionary hallucinations of youth, and disappointments of life, I would, if I could forget. But with a grateful mind, I welcome the fond memories that linger yet amid the laurel groves of Savannah, Georgia, whose ever green bowers shade the shell decked walks of the beautiful city.

One of the most pleasant memories in connection with the 1st Georgia Regiment was the presentation of a beautiful battle flag from the patriotic ladies of Savannah, Georgia, which I had the honor to receive for the Regiment. The flag was presented by Miss Carrie Bell Sinclair, the classic poetess of Savannah, Georgia; she will be remembered as the author of the "Homespun Dress" which is now often read with pride on patriotic occasions.

3

The distinguished guests from the city included Miss Jessie Cohen, Mrs. Sneed and her excellent husband, editor of the *Savannah News*, to whom we were greatly indebted for the success of the occasion; and now as hope shall brighten the days to come and 61 years yet, guilds the memory of the past to all whom it may concern.

After my six months' service as Sergeant Major of the 1st Georgia State Troops, our company re-enlisted in the Confederate Service for three years, or the war. We changed the name of our company from the Miller County Wild Cats to the Walker Rifles, and the company elected officers as follows:

B. R. Kendrick...........................Captain

R. D. Chapman...........................1st Lieutenant

James Lane.......................2nd Lieutenant

Thomas Sherfield...................3rd Lieutenant

The numerical strength of our company, rank and file, was 108 men. We were ordered to Griffin, Georgia, for regimental organization, and the Walker Rifles became Company E in the 55th Regiment, Georgia Volunteers, Confederate States Army, May the 3rd, 1862.

In June, 1862, we began active service, and while in front of General [Don Carlos] Buell's army on the Tennessee river, sickness prevailed to an alarming extent and very much reduced the efficiency of our army.

In anticipation of the Kentucky campaign the sick and disabled were sent to the rear; with the sick I was carried back to Atlanta, Georgia, where I remained thirty days in the family of Welden Mitchell on White Hall street, and was kindly cared for by his daughter, Mrs. Dr. Roach, to whom I owe a debt of gratitude. While in a convalescent condition I learned that General Bragg had ordered the Confederate army to advance into Kentucky. I had heard, read about, and dreamed of the Blue Grass Girls over in the old Kentucky home. The army was on the march; my doctor refused to let me go, but it was too good a trip to miss. I was stricken with a vision that bid me go or die; I bid defiance to the doctors and the importunities of friends, and started to my command hoping to join the army before it crossed the Cumberland mountains. The narrow gaps, the numerous cliffs and coves along the mountains were considered the danger points through which the army had to pass into Kentucky.

These places were infested with bushwhackers, bandits, out-laws and deserters from both the northern and southern armies, and often carried their murderous designs into execution and good citizens and soldiers were their victims. When I arrived at Knoxville, Tennessee, I received the sad news that my captain, B. R. Kendrick had been killed at one of the Cumberland Gaps, while enroute to the army. He joined ninety other mounted men, all armed and equipped for mutual protection on this perilous ride. They had been told that out-laws and robbers were in ambush waiting for all citizens and soldiers who would be worth robbing; this company of soldiers all had good horses, and they being mostly officers, financially prepared for the trip, were truly a rich find for their clan to execute their clannish designs, with the least danger to themselves. They secreted themselves among the rocks and cliffs over-hanging the route of travel, armed with their choice fire arms. As the company approached the gap under whip and spur they dashed into the rock-ribbed ravine hoping to out-ride the danger, and when well into the gap, both men and horses were shot to death in heaps and piles. How many men were killed history does not tell, and I do not know of any who escaped to tell the story.

The news of this tragedy came back to Knoxville and delayed our progress. Many soldiers arrived on every train, bound for Kentucky, and in three days we had mobilized six hundred soldiers for mutual protection, and started on our perilous march, not knowing what resistance we would encounter. We had but few guns in our company, therefore we sent out a scouting party to find the safest route into Kentucky; they reported that the Big Creek Gap route by the way of Jacksboro was the safest and most expeditious way to reach our commands in Kentucky. I joined my company at Camp Dick, Robinson, Kentucky, and was promoted from 1st Lieutenant to

Captain of the company the 12th day of September, 1862. After an active campaign in Kentucky, General [Braxton] Bragg ordered a general retreat, and the Army recrossed the Cumberlands; the 55th Georgia Regiment covered the retreat and halted at Cumberland Gap under the Command of General Gracy, where we remained during the winter of 1862.

The year 1863 resulted very disastrously to the 55th Georgia Regiment and many other commands of General Gracy's Brigade.

Our mountain campaigns were very hard and rough, but as yet we had not met with defeat or disaster, but in September, 1863, while holding the Gate Ways through the Cumberlands and protecting transportation between the eastern and western armies, General [Ambrose] Burnsides [sic; Burnside], commanding the ninth army corps advanced from the north and threatened our position. The Confederates concentrated their scattered detachments at Cumberland Gap and resisted the approach of the army. The Federals gathered around the mountain thick and fast with an overwhelming force which rendered further resistance impracticable. We had concentrated upon the lofty summit of Cumberland Gap mountain; this position we thought to be impregnable, but without supplies and munitions of war, no position can be impregnable. We formerly obtained our supplies from the surrounding country, but limited in supplies and ammunition, we could not hold out long without rations, or fight our way out through an army of ten to one. Our troops consisted of the 55th Georgia, an Alabama Regiment, a North Carolina Regiment, Infantry and the Laton Artillery of Atlanta, Georgia, all under the command of Brigadier General Frazier. On the 9th day of September, 1863, General Burnsides demanded our surrender. When the terms of the surrender were agreed upon and officially announced, the darkest gloom veiled the summit of that lofty mountain. Our faithful soldiers who had endured extreme hardships, and marched together through the dreadful consequences of war with a loyal devotion to duty were now victimized. The sun had withdrawn its cheerful rays from the lofty mountain peak of our occupation, and the near approach of night

6

rendered the scene still more appalling. Confusion, dismay and disgust, characterized the action and expression of every soldier, while the enemy, fifteen hundred feet in the valley below were flushed with victory.

Some of our brave soldiers who had faced danger on the battlefield were now weeping like children; others raging like mad men, while others in groups, were calmly discussing the situation.

Notwithstanding the terms of our surrender had been agreed upon and orders to cease firing had been issued to each command, Lieutenant McIntire commanding one section of the Laton Artillery continued to load and fire over the brink of a precipice down at the enemy, and when he was ordered the second time to cease firing, he threw his cannon, caisson and all over the precipice, and they went down crashing with such force as to remove thousands of huge rocks from their places on the slopes of the mountain, gathering in number and velocity, crushing everything down the mountain with irresistible force. The first relief of the enemy's picket line had been posted for the night along the foot of the mountain, and the reserve pickets were indulging in camp revelry, cooking and eating, and rejoicing over their bloodless victory, when they heard a noise as a mighty volcanic eruption followed by a great mass of earth, stone and timbers down into their midst. They fled in confusion regardless of their rations or picket duties. When this alarm was reported and investigated, the Federals tried to keep their stampede a profound secret, but it was too good a joke to keep; the next day one of the guardsmen told the joke and enjoyed the laugh that was coming to us. Lieutenant McIntire who created this confusion on the federal picket line, came to Texas after the war and became a prominent citizen of Dallas, Texas, and with the same indomitable will and push that dumped the cannon over the ill-fated brink, he accumulated an immense fortune and up to his recent death he enjoyed the full fruition of a life devoted to constructive progress.

The night succeeding our surrender passed in solitary gloom, greatly intensified by the thought of turning our backs upon home and loved ones, to a prison of hopeless despair. Preferring death upon the battle field, rather than submit to an ignominious surrender and languish indefinitely in a prison cell, I determined to make my escape by concerted action if possible while on the march, through Kentucky, a distance of more than a hundred miles.

The morning of the 10th of September, 1863, we were ordered down the winding declivity of the mountain into the open column of the victorious enemy. The rank and file were to march under guard, while the officers had the liberty of marching at will, if they preferred to do so. The officers of my company did not accept this generous offer, preferring to march with our company so that we might escape if possible without committing a breach of promise.

During the day and in the camp at night I worked with great energy among the prisoners to form a secret conspiracy against our guardsmen, overpower and disarm them, and thus secure arms for our protection and the accomplishment of desirable achievements which we had in view. On our second days' march we expected to meet a large supply train of one hundred wagons drawn by a great number of horses and mules, which we expected to capture and destroy after supplying ourselves with necessary equipments, mount the horses and mules, and make our escape through the mountains of southeast Kentucky.

This secret conspiracy to effect our escape had only been partially accomplished when we commenced meeting regiment after regiment of Federal troops as advance guard of the supply train, followed by a strong rear guard, which rendered the execution of my plans impossible. But whether I succeeded in liberating my company or not, I had never entertained the thought of entering the walls of a Federal prison to remain for an unlimited time without hope of exchange or release during the war, subject to the reckless arbitrament of war that tramples underfoot the sacred rights of the weak, and does not hesitate to wade through slaughter to conquest, and shut the gates of mercy on mankind.

This was the last day that the soldiers and officers could remain together; they were to be divided; the officers were ordered to Johnson's Island prison, the privates and non-commissioned officers were to be sent to Camp Douglass prison. The column halted for the night's encampment; our physical strength was very much depleted, and intensified by mental agony incident to our fatigue, unhappy and disappointed condition and hopeless future. Truly the supreme test that tries the souls of men had come. The last opportunity for a successful escape was now in view, but I did not feel physically able to make the venture alone. I made my intentions known to my first Lieutenant, James Lane, who was the embodiment of honorable impulses and heroic chivalry.

We were encamped in the semi-circle of a beautiful vine-clad creek where the prisoners were permitted to go for water to bathe and quench their thirst. Lieutenant Lane and I availed ourselves of this opportunity. Our modesty forbid a bathing in open view; we bundled up our clothing and sought a more private and convenient place. Finding ourselves unobserved by the guard, we pressed our way up the creek through a dense thicket securely protected from public view where we remained in concealment until after dark; our adventure thus far was very satisfactory, and the darkness of the night was favorable to further progress.

In leaving our hiding place it was of great importance that we avoid coming in contact with stragglers and foraging parties from the camps. We cautiously made our way to a mountain nearby, and climbed its rugged slope to its lofty peak that overlooked the prison camps in the valley below; this position was truly the most advantageous for our safety and placed us in full view of the camp fires of the prisoners and the picket guards, and gave us perfect protection against the approach of the enemy. Nestled in a cozy cavity at the base of a large rock surrounded by a jungle of natural growth, which we admired as much for its rural beauty as for its reclusive refuge.

As long as we gazed down upon our unfortunate comrades in prison bondage we could not realize that we were free, but when they struck tents the next morning and marched off toward prison as the band played 'The Girl I Left Behind Me"* in the dim distance we heard the thrilling strains of "Dixie" accompanied by the Rebel yell.

*Sung by soldiers of both armies.—Ed. 2016

Now the tumult and the music ceased, the captains and the soldiers had departed, and we began to realize our true situation; the time had come for decisive action and many details were to be considered.

First, we had only two hard tack crackers for our days' rations; second, our papers of identity must be destroyed; third, our proper names as recorded on the prison rolls could not be used; forth, we must have some business pursuit in view, should we be questioned about our business relations; fifth, the most serious consideration that confronted us was the disposition of our Uniform Coats decorated with gold lace showing the official rank of Captain and First Lieutenant of the Confederate army. My new uniform confederate gray coat was too valuable and comfortable to leave or destroy; I removed the gold lace, folded it with the black lining on the outside, tied it up in my towel and carried it as baggage. Lieutenant Lane's coat was not so valuable, but it was of very sacred memory; it was a homemade Jeans coat, spun and woven by his old mother; he carried his coat as I did mine.

We ate our two crackers for breakfast, destroyed our papers, changed our names, R. D. Chapman to Bob Whiteman, and James Lane to Jimmie Green, the School Teacher and the Farmer looking for a job. With eight dollars in Georgia State Bank money, a pocket knife, my sword belt, and our uniform coats as baggage I felt we could safely proceed. All details had now been worked out reasonably satisfactory; we were ready to explore an unknown region through the mountains of southeast Kentucky, hoping to reach Virginia or some other good country where we could resume our names and places in the Confederate army.

The Federal army occupied the country north, south and west of us and our only way of escape was through a mountainous country infested by out-laws and deserters from both armies. These out-laws organized themselves for protection against the law abiding citizens and often plundered his home, stole his horses, burned his house, and ordered him to leave the country or die. We did not realize the danger that awaited us.

10

On the 12th day of September, 1863, our travel was uninterrupted, except by fatigue and sore feet, until about 4 p m., after passing through a narrow gap in the mountain we came upon a crowd of men working on an old house. There was one idle, ragged, desperate-looking man on horseback talking to the crowd; we inquired of them the way eastward through the mountains and passed on our way. The man on horseback soon passed us, and turning out of sight we heard the clatter of his horses feet over the rock road as if in full speed. This together with the general fiendish appearance of the man, excited our suspicion but we were hemmed in so completely by mountains on each side of us, and the crowd we left behind, we could not change our direction. Encouraged by our successful escapade thus far during the day, we pressed on, trusting Providence for our safe journey through the rough and rocky gorges which became darker and more cheerless as the day declined.

Our mental agony, physical exhaustion, sore feet and hunger, challenged our serious consideration and detracted very much from the beautiful mountain scenery through which we were passing.

The mountains converged to a narrow valley; the sun had withdrawn its cheerful rays from the lofty cliffs on either side of us. The lonely hour of declining day intensified the fearful consequences of the coming night; daylight still favored our march as we approached a wonderful, but to us, a fearful natural scenery. The grim, gray mountain heights, over-shadowing the dark cavern into which we were about to enter, reminded us of the gateway to infernal darkness. Marching silently and slowly, single file along an unknown trail a rifle shot from an unknown source, answered by a shot ahead of us echoed and re-echoed through the mountain caverns, and before the sound of the shooting had died away we were confronted by six men armed with old mountain rifles who demanded our surrender.

Two other men soon joined the six, whom we supposed to be the men who did the shooting. Having been searched and surrounded by eight men, we at once recognized the man who preceded us a few hours before on horseback as one of the eight. They spirited us away through a divergent trail, way into a secluded mountain cove to a small log cabin. We did not know then that we were in the hands of the notorious Sizemore band of robbers who were afterwards represented to us as being desperate characters banded together in the mountains, regardless of humanity or personal rights, who left no living witnesses to testify to their atrocious crimes. This, and similar bands occupied a neutral zone between the northern and southern armies during the war between the states where neither army could subsist and where civilization could not exist. Far away from transportation and communication the mountain coves, cliffs and caverns furnished favorable retreats and hiding places for outlaws and deserters from both armies who would often rob, raid and terrorize the surrounding country within reach of their hiding places.

These bandits or similar characters known as bush-whackers had murdered our captain and many other soldiers from ambush in the mountains, whose bodies became the prey for vultures and carnivorous animals, and being fully aware of their clannish inhumanity, we had reason for fearing the same fate of our unfortunate comrades. They were the most hideous looking human beings we ever saw in the form of men; their long hair and beard, old flopped hats, ragged clothes, bare feet, filthy, savage appearance, all indicated the lowest type of humanity. Surrounded by this frightful band in front of a little old log cabin at that lonely twilight hour, it seemed to us that the gate of mercy had been closed upon us; hopelessness and despair supplanted the courage and valor that had cheered us on our way to this sad hour. We pleaded with them to let us go on our journey but they refused. As we entered the cabin for safe keeping, we beheld three women standing around the fire-place gazing at us, speechless as dummies; our mental and physical endurance languishing in the throes of exhaustion demanded rest, but seeing only two old chairs in the house and three women standing around, we stood and they stood and the two chairs stood until patience ceased to be a virtue and we sat down, and commenced talking to the old gray headed woman. She didn't remember her age but remembered the time when the stars fell; the two other women listened to our talk with interest; the guard at the door came in the cabin leaving his gun at the door and forgetting his duty as a guard, sat himself down on the floor in front of us, while the rest of the clansmen around the fire out in front of the cabin indulged in revelry and vociferous language. We knew we were in the hands of ruthless bush-whackers with but little hope of escape; we accepted the situation and played the role of agreeable companionship hoping to gain favor with them and save our lives.

The clan around the fire took possession of our bundles containing our uniform coats, unwrapped them, tried them on and appropriated them to their own use; my coat was a fine confederate gray uniform of the best style, make, and material, of which I was very proud; Lieutenant's coat was not so attractive and stylish but it was also captured, worn and kept by them as a prize. The most desperate one of this clan who had figured most conspicuously in our capture, wrapped himself in my fine military coat, forming a contrast too ridiculous to describe, acting as officer of the guard in military array. He was the subject of much hilarious criticism by the clansmen around the bonfire as they indulged in playful sport and vulgar language during the early part of the night.

The three women and the guard had become intensely interested in us and our conversation soon became general and attracted the attention of the clansmen around the fire in front of the cabin; one by one they approached the door of the cabin until they were all in, about, and around silently listening to our talk, and as we told story after story of living in the great cities, sea voyages, the chase and capture of wild animals in the jungles of Africa, they drew near around us with manifest pleasure and approbation. We observed that the clansmen had neglected the fire outside of the cabin and became deeply interested in the wonderful things spoken by the strange captives; we felt sure that this was our opportunity to gain favor with the clan, and we continued talking with all the eloquence we could possibly command. These bandits were our first auditors after assuming fictitious names. As I was known and recorded on the prison rolls as R. D. Chapman, Captain, Company E, 55th Georgia Regiment, to avoid identification as an escaped prisoner, I assumed the name of Bob Whiteman, and James Lane, 1st Lieutenant of the same command, assumed the name of Jimmie

Green, and we were soon known and spoken of by the clan as Bob and Jimmie. My friend Jimmie was a very modest unpretentious young man, slow of speech and with a stammering tongue, preferred to honor and obey rather than to lead his superiors in office; therefore I assumed leadership in planning and speaking as would best serve the demands of this occasion. I fully realized that this was our most propitious opportunity to enter into close communion with them, gain their good will and confidence. Accordingly I used every effort to overcome their antagonism, and establish a congenial companionship with them and while indulging freely in social equality, I carefully avoided all political expressions or questions that might lead to an investigation of our identity. We were not ready to make any kind of a confession until we knew more about our company. We had reason to believe that they held us as rebel spies or deserters from the Southern army, as our uniform coats and general appearance condemned us and we were fully aware of their antagonism, and expressed hatred of the rebel cause which they had freely expressed during the evening in threats of terror and death to their rebel enemies.

Thus having obtained a knowledge of their political proclivities and criminal characteristics, we were better prepared for an investigation, if they should demand our identity. The presence of their mysterious captives excited their curiosity to find out more about us, but we carefully avoided and evaded all of their questions and continued talking and singing for their entertainment until a late hour. Truly, I have never since been able to reproduce anything equal to that night's entertainment; my mental and physical endurance had about attained its limit; as yet no monotony prevailed.

The clansmen had stacked their guns about the cabin door and gathered around the cabin fire, manifesting a profound interest in the entertainment while the old lady sat near the fire smoking her pipe and indulging occasionally in exclamations of amazing wonder at the wonderful stories related by the speaker, whose loquacious resources could no longer respond to the demand of the occasion. It became necessary to change the program. Rising from my seat to catch a fresh inspiration I spied an old fiddle in a crack of the log cabin; I seized it with eager hands, pressing it to my bosom with expressions of affection and I found that I had struck their talent. Three of the clan volunteered their services to furnish music for the dance to conclude the nights entertainment; the fiddling, music and dancing was soon in progress in couples facing each other.

The eight clansmen and two of the women all participated in the dance each one keeping time to the music in their own peculiar manner. They were all bare-footed except the old woman; she had on an old pair of shoes which was used by the women dancers while on the floor. Fun and frolic of their choice style continued to a late hour. The old woman and the two prisoners had not yet participated in the dance; they had invited us several times to join them in the dance and we refused, but they insisted, and in order to excuse myself, I told them that my friend Jimmie was a good dancer. He had been trained to cut the pigeon wing, the highland fling, or the backstep in the wire grass region of Georgia, and at my request he took the floor facing one of the women and proved himself equal to the emergency, and very much to the edification of the clansmen.

All had contributed to the acrobatic activities of the entertainment except myself. On account of sore feet and other disabilities I excused myself several times during the night, preferring to sit in the corner and talk to the old woman, who was supposed to be too old to dance, but they insisted that I should dance, and at last I agreed to dance if the old woman would dance with me. She looked so thin and dilapidated I thought I would be safe in making that proposition but in a moment the old gray headed mountain mother stood erect before me; she stepped off to the music with the agility of a sixteen year old damsel. I faced her like a limber-jack, it was my first dance of that kind, and being right footed my left foot failed to keep time with the music, but she got there with both feet.

This was the closing performance of the night's entertainment.

Previous to this entertainment we expected to be executed during the night. A difference of opinion among them as to our fate was plainly indicated to us by the audacious implications and clannish secrecy that characterized their excited activities but during the entertainment the scale turned in our favor and we heard many expressions favorable to us which inspired the hope of seeing the dawn of another day.

At a late hour they placed a large sack of straw on the floor before the fire on which we retired. The guard resumed his post outside the door. The others resumed their places around the fire about twenty paces in front of the cabin door, where they continued their fun and frolic. When the light in the cabin had flickered out and all was dark within, the guard closed the cabin door and joined the clan around the fire. The loud talking and laughing ceased and they entered into a low, clannish conclave unintelligible to me. The light was gleaming through the cracks into the cabin through which I watched with eager eyes their movement so as to anticipate their designs. I could only hear enough of their talk to know that we were the subject of their discussion, I listened to catch an expression of their good or evil intent toward us, but their low clannish talk and excited gesticulations inclined me to believe that some clandestine plan was being arranged for our execution. In this dreadful state of mind, I saw them all rise to their feet, with a torch in hand and they said something about going over the mountain to the Cove. Four of them started with the light and four remained; the light soon disappeared. For an hour or two, silence reigned; my eyes were heavy but my mental vision still viewed the scene with sad solicitude. The solitude of the hour was broken by distant talking, and a light appeared upon the slope of the mountain. I watched the approaching light down the meandering trail of the mountain slope; it appeared nearer and nearer until its rays shot through the cabin cracks and I saw that their number had increased to six. On their return I listened and watched eagerly for the first word spoken and the first sign given. The first words I heard was a low depressing inquiry, "where are they?"

All right! said one. But to be sure of our presence or for some other reason they all advanced to the cabin door, opened it and cast their light upon our bed of straw. I arose to a reclining position, asked them if it was day, left Green in the cabin on the bed of straw and went out with them to the fire. I commenced talking about my friend

Green; I told them what a good man he was, a hard-working man, a good farmer, a good hunter; I was a school teacher. I talked to them about the best methods of teaching school until day. The day dawned dark and dreary, the cloud capped summits of the surrounding mountains, augmented the gloom and excluded the cheerful rays of the sun. My mind was yet clear, and my tongue responded to the demands of the occasion, but my physical nature was well near exhausted. The last square meal we had was afternoon on the 11th and the morning of the 13th of September, 1863, had dawned upon us and we had only five crackers and one pone of corn bread, which we appropriated to the best advantage. This insufficiency of food, physical exhaustion, and mental anguish, beggared description. The hours had become tedious and tasteless to me, sweet prospects, sweet birds, and sweet flowers had lost all their sweetness. My friend Green emerged from the cabin looking weary, friendless, and forsaken. The first thing I noticed was the hero of the band wearing my fine military coat with his bare feet and ragged legs, stepping about like a soldier upon the eve of a battle.

I went down to a little brook near-by to bathe my face for a morning refreshment. The guard with me intimated that he could possibly secure our release. I commenced pleading with him, and looking up toward the cabin I saw the military clansman and my friend Green coming to us, and the others of the clan coming towards us also. I anticipated at once their design; I was fully prepared to make a confession. They had expressed their hatred for the Rebels, their love for the Union and their opposition to the War. As they approached, the spokesman of the clan said to us, "Boys, we want you to tell us who you are; we think you are Rebels." Others joining in said, "Now boys, just come out and tell us the truth and pay us something and maybe we will turn you loose," or something to that effect. With an honest face and a tongue trained to righteous speaking, I said, "Yes, gentlemen, we have been Rebels. The truth has never hurt me, and I will give you a plain statement of facts. We were forced to join the Rebels and as soon as we got up into East Tennessee, we left them and come over here to keep out of the war. I will tell you how it is down south. All the men, old and young have to go to war." The clan listened and looked approvingly; I continued;

"We did not want to fight against the old union, and we left the Confederate army and came over here in the mountains to keep out of the war, and get some work to do by which we can make a living, and if we have to fight we will fight for the old Union. This cruel war was gotten up by the big, rich men, and the poor fellows have to leave their homes to fight for them and their negroes. We are not thieves or criminals; we are here seeking employment; we did not expect to be taken up here; we are strangers, and did not know where else to go." After a brief talk as above outlined, we returned to the cabin, and found the women grating corn on a tin grater, to make bread for breakfast, there being no mills in that country. We were very much interested in breakfast as we had only eaten the said five hardtack crackers and a loaf of corn bread in about fifty-two hours, and it was getting to be a serious matter with us. We offered our services to assist the women in grating the corn; they turned the job over to us, and we pushed up the business. We soon had enough Corn-Husk to start the old woman to cooking. The corn was green corn but too hard for roasting ears, and tasted very palatable, and while Green grated the corn, I gnawed the cob, and Green would have filled his stomach with the husk also, but his modesty prevailed. We had corn-husk bread and some kind of wild meat for breakfast and it was good.

After breakfast the man wearing my coat wanted to know what we would give them to let us go on our way. He already had on my fine uniform coat. I surrendered eight dollars in Georgia State money and a pocket knife; I had two hundred dollars in Confederate money which they did not get.

Now the robbery was complete and I indulged some hope of our freedom, but when I found that two of the most desperate characters of the clan, were to go into the mountains with us to show us the way, I began to doubt their motives. They discharged their rifles and reloaded them. They started and we followed two or three hundred yards to the point of a high, narrow ridge between two ravines. They directed us to go to the left and they started up the ravine on the opposite side of the ridge. Their pale criminal faces, their manner of speech, their light un-natural steps as they started off, expressed their criminal intent. I was satisfied that they intended to intercept us and shoot us from the mountain.

I had served in the army of east Tennessee two years among the mountains and was often charged with the duty of dislodging robbers, and bushwhackers, from the cliffs and coves, my Captain B. R. Kendrick was shot to death while passing through a mountain gap, by these dreadful characters. They never killed a man in open combat, in presence of witnesses. The sound of their well-aimed rifle was always heard from their hiding places; I understood their methods of war-fare. We fully believed they had' set a trap for us, and to follow their direction would prove fatal. We had only gone two or three hundred yards as they directed us. What shall we do? No time for discussion. The cabin of the clan left behind were almost in sight, the riflemen just over the ridge, rushing to the supposed point of execution. Physically wrecked and run down, sore feet, almost bare-footed, no rations; all would have been things of serious consideration in anticipation of an ordinary Mountain Campaign. But here, immediate action was necessary, and as the senior officer, I ordered a quick flight, by the left flank, double quick march into the thicket. Up the rugged mountain's slope, on, and still onward we tramped silently and cautiously through the thicket, upon rough, rocky slopes, beneath lofty cliffs and upon the brink of precipices. It was a dark, cloudy day; we had no sunshine, compass or chart, to direct our march.

Thus we wandered all day with no other object in view than to escape the possible pursuit of the robbers. We were lost; we could not go far in any direction until we were confronted by a wall of rock or standing upon a precipice, forcing us to change our direction. We therefore did not know the direction from which we came or wither we were going, but we reasonably concluded that we were a safe distance from the clan who had entertained us the last night, and we sat down to rest our weary limbs.

Through many dangers, toils and snares we had already come, but where to go and what to do was the problem to solve. We were in a very secluded spot, where it seemed that the foot of man had never trod, a kind providence conducted us to this beautiful spot for needful rest and meditation. And while amid the convulsive throes of our struggle for life and liberty, nature in all its magnificence and grandeur yielded a sweet relief and mitigated our sorrow. An hour's rest gave relief to our mental and physical condition, but hunger and sore feet demanded our serious consideration. We could forego and endure the hunger, as we had done often times before, but our sore feet was a torture to the flesh every step. My friend was a strong, healthy man, and well shod, but I had traveled part of the day neither bare-footed or shod; one of my shoe-soles had ripped to the heel, and went flipty flop every step; no knife to cut—no strings to tie—and no time to stop. I pulled it off and marched one sock and one shoe. This made a bad thing worse, and I put the sock over the shoe sole, foot and all. GOD BLESS CONFEDERATE WOMEN, for knitting such socks. It was now late in the evening; we had marched all day on the mountains to avoid the little foot trails in the valleys for fear of meeting some of the Clan, but as night was approaching, we decided to descend the mountain and find a path in which we could travel during the night until we got out of our bewildered condition. Accordingly we soon found a well-trodden path in which we walked rapidly a few minutes, and found ourselves in sight of the cabin and at the very same place where we parted with the two robbers in the morning. We at once recognized the place and realized our situation; confusion and dismay fell upon us and in breathless silence we beat a rapid retreat.

I had been leading all day in the mountain march, but now Lieutenant Lane, or so-called Jimmie Green took the lead, jumping logs across the paths, and heading straight away down the ravine without regard to the crookedness of the path, while I being tender-footed, had to crawl over the logs and follow the meanderings of the path. Jimmie possessed great physical force, and fast on foot, left me far behind; my helpless condition required more cunning and strategy, and less speed. It has been said, that the race is not always to the swift or the Battle to the Strong, but this was an exception to the adage. I had lost command of my lieutenant, who had gone down the valley like a wild ox. I too, became a little demoralized in my deserted condition, and hurried up a little, and was passing where Jimmie had stopped in, a thicket near my path, "Halt!" said he in a low, sharp voice. I jumped behind a tree, and expected a shot from the clan until I saw Jimmie emerging from the thicket.

It was dusky twilight when in my mental vision the stumps and trees looked like men, I again took the lead and advanced cautiously along the dark valley trail. We were very hopeful now, for we were not lost as we had been all day; we had located the Robbers Den and had turned our backs upon them and felt that we had passed our greatest danger. With the night before us in which to gain a place of safety.

We traveled east as we had been directed. The early part of the night was very dark and we had some trouble at South-Fork Creek; we crossed Cut-Shin Creek, and later in the night we waded Red Bird River and about three o'clock in the morning of September 14, we came in sight of a barn and a field which looked more like civilization. Here our human endurance completely failed, and we stopped to rest, make a good, hot fire, dried our clothing, went to a barn and slept in the wheat straw. We slept very soundly until late in the morning; while we slept the farmer passed by going up the creek to mill; he stopped and saw to his great displeasure that somebody had been burning his rails; he passed on, and we slept until late in the morning. We left our bed of straw and with empty stomachs and sore feet traveled eastward, passing the farmer's house near the road. We inquired of his boy the way we should go. The direction in which we were traveling should lead us to a Rebel settlement by or before night where we expected to find some sympathizers. Lawlessness and sectional strife ran very high here during the War; one Band raiding the country, burning houses, driving out horses and cattle, and another antagonizing Band, retaliating. And the more law abiding citizens were forced to organize the Union Home Guards, for protection of person and property.

The said Farmer belonged to the Home Guards, and when he returned home from the mill his little boy told him of two men passing by in the direction of the Rebel settlement. He concluded we were two of the Rebel raiders, and he and another citizen armed and equipped themselves and pursued us. In consequence of hunger, weakness and sore feet, we had made slow progress that day. Our pursuers traveled a nearer route across a mountain, intercepted our march, secreted themselves in a thicket near the road and awaited our coming. When I had almost reached the extreme limit of human endurance, and in full view of the mountain, upon whose summit we expected to find peace, and plenty, a rush from the thicket attracted our attention and two men stood with presented guns demanding our surrender. I felt that it would have been better for me had they shot me dead on the spot. But our captors advanced with their guns presented, and seeing that we made no resistance, they recovered arms, and one of them advanced and searched us for arms, and finding none the farmer said. You are not the fellows we expected to find but you are Rebels. "Yes," said I, "We have been, but we are not now," presuming that they were Union Men, and perhaps connected with the Sizemore Clan, who had so recently entertained us, we could not afford to make a contradictory statement.

The farmer said it was fortunate for us that we did not reach the Mountain one mile ahead. That we would have been shot by the Rebel Bush-Whackers and he urged us to return quickly to a place of safety. We asked for a short time to rest, but they refused, saying, they were now on forbidden ground and would be pursued if seen by their Rebel enemy. I rested upon the ground indifferent to their fearful importunities, preferring to be on the firing line between them, than to start back over the rugged road to the farmer's place, and in the direction of the Sizemore Band. In my sick, helpless, hopeless condition, I did not feel able to go, after making a statement of my condition to them, they expressed some sympathy for me, and said they had a horse tied in the woods beyond the mountain and proposed to let me ride. They soon got the horse and I together, and we journeyed on back to the farmer's house that we passed in the morning, and where a good warm supper awaited us at nine o'clock that night. This was on the night of the 14th of September, at 9, and was the first time we had eaten since nine a m. on the 12th, 36 hours fasting, and marching, over rough mountain road created an abnormal appetite. Upon our arrival at the farmer's house great excitement prevailed in the large family, from infancy to old age, they supposed the father to be in pursuit of Rebel Bandits.

The safe return of the father from his perilous pursuit relieved their fearful apprehensions, and a pleasing curiosity anxiously awaited further developments. We were now only nine miles from the Sizemore Band, and the news of our robbery and escape had reached the farmers family during the day. They had no telegraphs or telephones in that country, but they had women there, and a woman carried the news to the farmers family, and gave in detail our experience with the Sizemore Band and our mysterious escape.

The news was soon communicated to the farmer and he demanded an explanation of us. He inquired of us concerning the robbery, but I evaded his inquiry, having learned that his name was Sizemore also, and perhaps related to the Sizemore Band. I told him that we had been taken up by some men by the name of Sizemore, and treated badly by them. I did not want to tell anything about it. We wanted to get out of the country with as little trouble as possible, where we could travel without being taken up every day.

This did not satisfy farmer Sizemore. He wanted the truth and the whole truth. All about the robbery and he guaranteed to us perfect protection.

I gave him our names, Bob Whiteman and Jimmie Green, as we had given to the robbers, and proceeded to relate in detail, our experiences with the Sizemore Band. Farmer Sizemore had treated us with sympathetic care from our first acquaintance we could no longer doubt his sincerity, and I told him what had been taken from us by the robbers, and our fearful experience during our so join with them. He denounced them as out-laws, thieves and robbers and continued telling of the atrocious crimes they had committed. He expressed his surprise that our lives had been spared as living witnesses of their robbery. I told him the half of my story had not yet been told, and perhaps the untold part of our strategic movement would explain our successful escape.

I related the story of our escape from the two desperadoes who escorted us to the point of a mountain ridge and directed us to the left while they, well-armed and equipped, started their way, and when out of sight, our suspicion of their murderous designs, inclined us to disregard their directions and fly to hiding places upon the mountain.

"Now, I understand" said he, "your flight into the thicket, defeated their criminal designs and saved your lives, it was a profitable days work, you are the only men known to pass that way alive, during the lawless period of the Civil War."

They left no living witnesses, and dead men could not testify.

Farmer Sizemore was a cousin to the robbers, but was an excellent gentleman and a good citizen. The same is true in regard to the man who assisted him in our capture, whose name we did not learn.

Farmer Sizemore denounced the robbers in bitter terms, and declared we should have our stolen goods returned to us. I protested against that and begged him to abandon any effort to recover the stolen goods, and avoid if possible bringing us in contact with the robbers. He assured us that there would be no danger, and we need not fear while under his protection. Notwithstanding his promise of protection, we feared the result, and we could not persuade him to desist from his purpose.

We placed ourselves under his protection, and asked his advice, that we might be placed under more favorable circumstances. He advised us to go to the Federal authorities at Mansfield or Boonsville and take the oath of allegiance to the Federal Government and procure papers to travel at will, in order to get protection out of that country to a place of safety. As he was an officer we agreed to his suggestion. The fact is we were prisoners, but had we been free, we were not able to pursue our journey without assistance.

He and another man procured two horses to transport four men and made ready to start. We started early next morning (the 15th of September), to the Federal authorities ostensibly to take the oath of allegiance. It was 20 miles to Boonsville, Kentucky, where this performance was to take place. I rode one of the horses, and the three other men rode one horse alternately. It was a rough and rugged road to travel and led us directly back by the place where we had been robbed of our goods two days before.

We arrived in sight of the Sizemore cabin about 10 a m., one of our escort called for them to come out and only one of the Clan appeared. Our friend, Farmer Sizemore demanded the goods and the robbers surrendered our coats without resistance and received a scathing reprimand from our farmer friend, and to my surprise and satisfaction we passed on in safety, arriving at our place of destination that evening.

A great crowd gathered around us and followed us to the hotel. The news spread rapidly over the little town.

After supper the crowd gathered in and around the hotel. Provost Marshall and Col. Lucas of the 10th Regiment of Kentucky Cavalry, Farmer Sizemore and others, all were waiting with amazing wonder, in anticipation of what, how, and when something would happen. Now was my time to speak. I faced the official gentlemen, looking them squarely in the face and asked them if they were Federal Officers. "I am the Provost Marshall here" said one, "and my name is Lucas, Colonel of the 10th Kentucky Cavalry," said the other.

"I am glad to know you gentlemen" said I, "my name is R. D. Chapman, Captain of Company E, 55th Georgia Regiment, Confederate States Army, and this gentleman is my 1st Lieutenant, same company and regiment."

"We were captured at Cumberland Gap by General Burnsides army. We escaped from captivity, and in trying to travel through the mountains and rejoin our army, we fell into the hands of a band of robbers. We represented ourselves as Rebel deserters, and assumed fictitious names, and by using a little strategy we made our escape from the robbers, and the next day were arrested by these gentlemen, who brought us hither to take the oath of allegiance. We have made an honest effort to escape and we have failed to do so, and now we ask your most favorable consideration, not as Rebel deserters, but as prisoners of war as true to our Confederate cause and our Southern homes as you are to yours, and we only ask to be treated as prisoners of war.

Col. Lucas listened with interest and as I related the troubles and hardships through which we had passed, he seemed enthused with our patriotic devotion to principle, and his great heart swelling with magnanimity, and overflowing with sympathetic emotion. He assured us of his protection and personal friendship. He said we had acted the part of brave honorable soldiers and should receive such respect as was due a prisoner of war.

The Colonel was one of the old Kentucky type of American gentlemen. We talked over the political situation until a late hour at night. This was the first night's sleep we had enjoyed since our capture, Six days and nights under extreme mental and physical strain which had reduced me to a helpless condition. On the 16th of September, we were carried back to London, Kentucky, within six miles of where we first escaped and delivered to the officers of the 11th New Hampshire Regiment and from there we were sent, under guard, to Louisville, Kentucky prison, where we remained 10 days. John Willie of the 11th New Hampshire Regiment, was one of the guards who escorted us from London to Louisville, and distinguished himself by treating us with great kindness. He was afterwards captured by the Confederates and I found him in the Andersonville prison. I took him out and paid him three fold for his kindness to me when I was sick and in prison. I will refer to him again. From Louisville we were sent with three of Morgan's men, under guard, to Johnson's Island, a Federal prison in Lake Erie, near Sandusky City, Ohio. On our way to Johnson's Island it was necessary to stop at Indianapolis, Indiana to await train connections, and we were put in purgatory, three hours for safe keeping. Our officer of the guard was a very good man, and proposed to vouch for us, but the jailer was an old devil, and as he forced us into the prison door, a stench of human filth gushed out, and with an oath he said it was good enough for our sort.

The floor was slimy, the crowd was fiendish, and the stench was intolerable. The desperadoes called us fresh fish; they gathered around us threatening to take our clothing and divide among themselves. We backed up in a corner. One bold fellow ventured up and put his hand on the shoulder of one of the Morgan men, and he gave him a kick and a lick, and sent him winding through the crowd and he didn't come to time anymore. After three hours detention at Indianapolis we resumed our journey.

Distinguished Visitors

We arrived at Johnson's Island September 30th, 1863, and were located in Block No. 9, among strangers. Prisoners were located according to their date of arrival, hence we were separated from the officers of our regiment who had preceded us. Our prison comrades were mostly Missourians who were captured on Island No. 10. They were very agreeable companions and some were men of distinction in the persons of Breckenridge and Wooley of Kentucky; Choctaw and other from Indian Territory.

Johnson's Island was in the southwest part of Lake Erie, between Ohio and Canada, near Sandusky City. The prison enclosure contained 7 or 8 acres and 2500 or 2600 officers were held as prisoners of war, who were composed of the best talent of the South; the professions of Law, Physic, Theology, Mechanism and Agriculture were all represented. The prison walls were about 18 feet high, with an elevated parapet on the outside for the sentinel's beat. The walls were made of plank of considerable thickness and strength; the prison quarters were of rough plank on the box house style, about 80 feet by 25 feet, with a partition across the center, a door on each side of the partition and a ten foot cook room at each end of the building. These buildings were two story; the upper story of the same dimensions and capacity as the lower story; each room accommodated thirty men a large stove was used for heating in each room, and a cook stove in each cook room. The allowance of wood in cold weather would last generally, until nine o'clock at night. The sleeping bunks were made of rough plank three by six feet, one above the other from the floor to the ceiling; a sack of straw in the bunk and two blankets were furnished for each man and two men slept in one bunk. Our rations were reasonably good for a prison fare, and in sufficient quantity except when the lake would freeze over and the ice began to thaw, so that neither wagons or boats could travel. At short intervals our rations ran short, our clothing was very insufficient for that climate, and we suffered extremely of cold, some becoming frost bit and many contracting disease, resulting in death. During my stay on the island from the 30th of September to the 9th day of February, 1864, was said to be a period of the coldest weather that had been experienced in many years. The dead house was an awful sight, 20 or 30 men laid out in a frozen state for a week or ten days and often buried in a watery grave.

Diphtheria and pneumonia were the prevailing diseases on the island. During the winter, several of my friends stricken with these dread diseases, were taken out to the hospital; they all died, and were laid out in the dead house. I was also taken sick with this fatal disease, and grew worse daily. I thought of the dead house, and in my mental vision I could see many other hideous things incident to a death in a prison bunk on a bed of straw. As all my comrades who had been sent to the hospital had died, I decided to take my chances in my bunk among my friends, under the kind treatment of Dr. Scales of the 55th Georgia Regiment, and when in my greatest distress, I received the following letter from a good lady in Kentucky, which will explain itself:

Louisville, Ky., October 25th, 1863.

Captain Chapman,
Sir:—
My husband has just received a letter from you stating that yourself and two or three others in being captured lost your clothes, etc. If you will send me your size I will send the clothes to you by express. Please write what you are in need of and I will send them to you.
Yours respectfully,

Elizabeth Owens.

This was the first letter I had received in prison, and it filled my heart with gratitude over-flowing, to think this good woman would remember me so kindly when sick and in prison. I turned, facing the wall, took a good cry. I felt relieved and commenced improving and recovered. I answered this kind letter and in a short time I received the following:

Louisville, Ky., Nov. 7th, 1863.

Captain Chapman,
Sir:—
I received your letter yesterday and hasten to reply. I send you a suit of underwear for yourself, and also a suit for Lieutenants Lane and Sheffield,

all sent by the Rev. J. B. English, to whom you wrote. He wishes you to write to him and let him know if you get the clothing safely. I send you nine dollars in money—three for yourself, three for Lieutenant Lane and three for Lieutenant Sheffield, all sent by Rev. Mr. English... He wishes you to write to Mr. Richard Simmons, Charles Lee and Ham Fields, all of Shepardville, Bullit County, Kentucky, and they will assist you when needed.

I hope you will bear your confinement with fortitude, looking forward to a speedy exchange, and when this cruel war is over if you should ever visit our city call on us.

Please write, although we have never had the pleasure of seeing each other it is pleasant to correspond.

Very respectfully,

Elizabeth Owens.

I continued to improve and soon regained my health. About this time the Federals refused to let us write to anyone except relatives and I wrote to aunt Elizabeth Owens, and soon received a reply as follows:

Louisville, Ky., Dec. 19, 1863.

Capt. R. D. Chapman,
Dear Nephew:—
I received your letter of the 3rd, which is the first I have heard of you in some time. I received the beautiful ring you sent me and shall keep it sacred to the memory of one whom I esteem as a relative and a friend. Please accept my heartfelt thanks for it. All join in love to you.

Your affectionate aunt,

Mrs. Elizabeth Owens.

In due time I received another letter from this good woman, dated

Louisville, Ky., Jan. 4, 1864.

Capt. R. D. Chapman,
Dear Nephew:—
I received yours yesterday and I am very glad to hear you are recovering your health. Do try and take care of yourself. I regret exceedingly you did not let me know sooner you needed clothing; I would have sent them long since. I want you to send me your size for clothing and shoes, and I will send you a box in care of Col. Piersons.

Mr. Simmons and Mr. English have not heard from you yet, write to them for money, you will get it.

I feel very uneasy about you this cold weather. I know you all have suffered. Now my dear child do not hesitate to let me know what you need, for I know you could get what you need at your home, although you are far away from your home don't forget that I am not so far from you, but what I can assist you, I will do cheerfully, I could talk to you all day, but as we are limited I will stop.

Your aunt,

Elizabeth Owens.

Oh! Thou Angel of Mercy, I was hungry and ye gave me meat, thirsty and ye gave me drink, a stranger and ye comforted me, naked and ye clothed me, and when sick and in prison ye administered unto me.

More than 58 years have elapsed since I was the grateful recipient of these kind letters from Mrs. Elizabeth Owens (whom I have never seen or heard from since). Yet through all these years of eventful travels and trials, I have preserved these letters, sacred to the memory of this good woman. If she still lives and her eyes should ever fall upon these lines, may it please her to know that the little ring sent her and held sacred to the memory of a Georgia soldier, was given me as a token of love by a patriotic daughter of Georgia, who died while I was in prison. She placed the ring upon my finger and bade me go and return with honor or never return.

If she is dead, her deeds still live as triumphal arches of human charity.

I remained on Johnson Island from the 30th day of September 1863 to February 9th, 1864. We were occasionally subjected to unauthorized insults and abuse which was very common in all prisons, and was generally the result of disobedience of orders. A bad disobedient prisoner invites ill treatment, and a mean cowardly guard is generally insulting and abusive to his prisoner. A truly brave honorable soldier is always moved in the cause of humanity for his prisoner, guards him securely and protects him from all harm. I have been in prison and I have had a great many prisoners under my control, and it is my experience with but few exceptions, that-the officers commanding prisons, north and south, were magnanimous, sympathetic men, but they were of necessity, very strict disciplinarians. The free American soldier makes a very bad prisoner, compared with prisoners of other nationalities. He loves personal liberty and don't like to be restrained; they are very resentful while in prison and require a strict rule and often severe punishment. He will keep his parole of honor within prison bounds, but he rebels against despotic rule even in a prison cell, and if there is one chance in a thousand for his liberty he will take that chance.

There were many conspiracies and secret conclaves organized among the prisoners to escape from the island, but their plans were generally detected by secret spies. Several prisoners escaped from the prison walls by bribing guards and digging tunnels, but found themselves water-bound on the island. When the lake was frozen over they crossed on the ice, hoping to reach Canada, but they were re-captured and returned to prison in a frozen condition, resulting in amputation of limbs and often death.

The most amusing, unsuccessful effort to escape was led by Captain Chappell and his confederates. They dug a tunnel under the west end of the southwest block and had been at work faithfully a long time, using case knives for digging and tin cans for removing earth. They completed the tunnel in about three months. When the low level of the tunnel was passed a flood of water collected in the tunnel behind the digger, and rendered it difficult of ingress and egress, but inspired with the hope of freedom, they pursued their work with vigor until they completed it, but did not dare break through the surface until an opportune time.

All things now being ready, the dark night favored their escape from the prison walls, but the water of Lake Erie still held them in prison bounds.

They expected to escape from the island by a raft of logs. Captain Chappell was the first hero of the hole; he bid his friends farewell, and made a head-on plunge into the hole, struggling through mud and water, broke through, crawled out and slipped away. The next heroic adventurer, ready, waiting and watching for the result of Chappell's escape, after waiting a sufficient time, he crawled down into the mud and water, and found the way clear.

31

Other prisoners followed until nine had escaped, the tenth man was a large man with broad hips and a considerable bay window, and with a resolution as big as himself, he tackled the hole, but stuck fast in the small part of the tunnel. The more he struggled to extricate himself the closer old mother earth held him in her fond embrace. In that extreme torture he patiently held his peace in silence until broad daylight, in order to give his comrades time to escape. Then his voice rang out as a swift messenger from the dark caverns of hades. The prisoners and the Federal Guard were thrown into confusion, and great excitement prevailed.

An investigation was ordered, the hole was found, and cause of the alarm reported, to the authorities, the body was located about midway the tunnel. Sympathizing friends were volunteering their services and urging the Federals to give relief to suffering humanity. They were strolling around in a dilatory manner, tickled to death at the Rebel yells from the bowels of the earth.

When the excitement was highest and the work of relief begun, the prison gates flew open, and the nine who preceded the victim, came marching back into prison, besmirched with muddy slush from head to foot.

The cries of the unfortunate comrade grew weaker, and as the work of relief approached near the body, the loose earth broke in and rendered his relief almost hopeless. He was saved, although almost dead. This unsuccessful effort to escape was the source of much amusement among the prisoners, of which the poets wrote and sang, for the entertainment of both Confederates and Federals, to the tune of Gidians Band.

I conceived the idea that I could improve upon the experience of my unfortunate friends by digging a tunnel as they did and escape when the lake was covered with ice. The lake would freeze over very often, and any one accustomed to ice navigation could make good their escape, but the majority of the southern soldiers could not travel on ice. I had never tried the ice navigation, but I understood how to dig holes in the ground. Two of my comrades joined me in the enterprise. We equipped ourselves with knives and tin cans.

We advised the cook of our plans and secured the use of the slop hole in the floor of the cook room through which we could descend to the ground under the house. I dropped down through the greasy hole and landed in a great pile of garbage. I crawled around, surveyed the situation, and commenced the tunnel directly under the large cook stove for protection in extreme cold weather. I prescribed a circle of five feet in diameter and commenced the work in a systematic order. My confederates and I alternately divided the time of labor equally. The hope of success overcame the torture of blistered hands and other inconveniences, and the work progressed very well during the first and second days. The morning of the third day I was hard at work, and while meditating over the prospective cost of liberty, a message was handed down through the slush hole, that we were ordered to leave the island. I suspended business to investigate the authenticity of this new order. I ascertained that we were to be shipped from Johnson Island to Point Look-out, in alphabetical order ABC and D in the first shipment.

I turned over my interest in the tunnel to my partners, and prepared for the new route south, having free transportation part of the way. All kinds of rumors were circulated among the prisoners; they could not understand why just 400 prisoners were to be carried to Point Look-out. The most prevailing opinion was, that they were to be held as hostages for retaliation.

The prison department of Maryland was commanded by General Butler, very unfavorably known throughout the south as Beast Butler the Tyrant, Spoon Thief. The dark side of General Butler's character had been presented to us as being void of humanity, and we deplored the idea of being placed under his command. I determined to make my escape while in transit, before reaching General Butler's department.

I had no definite plan of escape, but I intended to employ every agency and take every chance to escape regardless of results.

To make my escape more possible, I sought to secure a small saw kept and used in the curiosity shop by an ingenious workman who had collected quite a supply of Tinker's tools; he had two small saws on his work-bench, and relying upon his patriotic generosity, I applied to him for one of his saws. My request was promptly met by an insulting denial. I left him in disgust. Soon the Federal officers appeared on the parapet over the gate, and commenced calling the roll in alphabetical order, commencing with A, all the prisoners whom the order of exit applied, had assembled at the gate, ready, waiting to step out when their names were called. As the roll call progressed the remaining prisoners assembled to bid their departing comrades an affectionate farewell. The Tinker who had refused me the use of one of his saws left his work-bench, and went out to see his friends off; taking the advantage of his absence I stepped back to the prison house and swiped both of his saws, placing the saw blade in my shoe quarter and the handle up my pants leg.

Thus with a Tinker's saw in each pants, leg, I bid my friends good bye, and when my name was called I stepped out with a clear conscience, and should the Tinker ever charge me with theft of his two little saws, I would plead limitation, deny the allegation and demand the proof.

This was the 9th day of February, 1864. We were marched to the Ferry Boat, crossed lake Erie and landed at Sandusky City, and quartered that night in the Armory, under a strong guard and I saw no way of escape.

On the 10th we were transported down through Ohio. During the night of the 10th I used one of my little saws freely on the floor of the car in the vain hope of cutting my way out through the bottom but the little saw, inadequate to the accomplishment of such a tough job of work, became very much dilapidated and unfit for use; I reserved my best saw for future use. Soon after the day guards found the hole, which very much resembled a thunderbolt tearing its way through a solid wall. The seat near the hole was vacated but my baggage was left under the seat. A guard was placed over the hole and ordered to guard the baggage, while others were searching for the saw that did the work, and threatening to punish the workman if found.

34

To prevent a further search for the saw I slyly slipped the old bent up saw out on the floor of the car where it could be easily found. They soon found it and discontinued the search.

I still had my best saw securely hid, but they had my satchel under guard which was a source of trouble and suspense to me; the owner of the satchel was supposed to be the guilty party who sawed up the car.

The guard on duty was a wide awake, watchful, young fellow and kept vigilant watch over my baggage, but the relief guard came on in due time, and a dull looking thick headed fellow was placed on guard. I soon engaged him in conversation, took a seat by him, directly over my satchel. I continued talking to him about natural scenery and other things, to divert his attention, and at an opportune time I drew my feet up quickly under the seat, kicked my satchel back within easy reach of my friends, sitting just behind me. The boys were all watching my movements and were ready to assist me in regaining my baggage, and prevent my punishment, if identified as the rascal who sawed up the car. They slyly slipped my satchel back from seat to seat until it was safely hidden away with other baggage. I still remained on the seat with the guard, telling him of old times in Georgia. The sergeant with the relief guard entered the car, rushing down the aisle. At the approach of the new relief, the old guard arose to his feet, they faced each other presented arms, (I retained my seat between them.) The old guard proceeded to transmit his instructions to the new guard, here is the hole, but where is the satchel, said the new guard. They looked under the seat, and I looked under the seat, but the little satchel could not be found, and the poor guard was sent out under condemnation for dereliction of duty. This was quite amusing to the prisoners and a great relief to me. Thus ended the 11th day of February, 1864.

Late in the evening we stopped at Harrisburg, Pa., and drew one days rations. As usual, this day's ration was consumed the first meal.

All plans and efforts to escape had failed, and this was the last night before reaching Point Lookout Prison from which there was no chance of escape.

My determination to escape had not abated; I had learned that "Eternal vigilance is the price of liberty."

Though the night was dark and cold, and life itself poised upon the perilous venture, yet the light in the window of hope had not grown dim; the irrevocable decree had gone forth and from it there was no appeal. This night must settle the issues of liberty or death.

I made my intentions known to a few friends. Captain T. I. Ball of Cuthbert, Ga., gave me five dollars in gold; Lieutenant Bowling gave me valuable information as to the geography of the country. He was wounded in the battle of Gettysburg and while in hospital, a party of charitable ladies of

Emmetsburg, Md., visited the sick and wounded soldiers at Gettysburg, Penn. Miss Annie McBride, one of the ladies, and Lieut. Bowling became confidential friends. He gave me her name and informed me that her father was an old Roman Catholic and a true Southern man.

Emmetsburg was about 35 miles from the railroad in a westerly direction, and York, on the Pennsylvania Central, was the place where I expected to escape from the train.

My escape had to be made through the window of the car while in motion. At every stop the guards on the platform would step down and form a line of guard on each side of the train, and when the train started they resumed their places on the platforms. This rendered my escape more perilous, as I could have no choice where or how I would land. It was 10 o'clock at night; most of the prisoners were asleep, but those who were advised of my intention, were wide awake, and it was understood when the train stopped at York, they would have their blankets unfolded so that they might fix for rest and sleep; and when the whistle blew for York, every fellow commenced spreading down his blanket, and if he didn't have a blanket of his own he got somebody's blanket or overcoat and joined the blanket brigade. As the train pulled out amid the blanket confusion I slipped out, my left leg and body, holding firmly to the window sill, and in the struggle to keep my head from going first, my right foot refused to clear the window. Thus clinging to the side of the car, head in one side of the window and one foot in the other side, I extended my arms, lowered my body; my foot cleared the window and I turned loose; and then, thunder and lightning, earthquake, dirt, dust and blood—all were in evidence, but my mind was clear and no bones broken. I remained as I had fallen until all the train of cars had passed; the fall did not hurt me as much as striking the ground, my feet first, then my head, shoulder, and arms; they were badly lacerated.

The excitement of my friends and the guard with uplifted gun glittering in the light, pressing forward, presented a scene that time can never erase. The train had passed a short distance, the guard reported my escape and the train stopped; another train came approaching me from the rear reflecting its headlight toward me; I realized my perilous position, arose and retreated rapidly at right angles from the railroad.

Dazed, dusty and bleeding, the headlight from the approaching train so confusing my vision, that my progress was quite difficult in the dark. I soon found myself upon the slope of a mountain, overlooking the town. The Federal guards came back looking for the escaped prisoner while I was resting securely and watching the movements of their signal lights. They gave up the search, returned to their train and pursued their journey, carrying my comrades to a prison of hopeless despair where they remained until the end of the war. Truly I felt, friendless and forsaken. It was the lonely hour of a dark, cold night, February 11th, of 1864, a lone Confederate soldier had invaded Pennsylvania, flanked the enemy, and gained an eminence overlooking the city of York, and from that lofty position I surveyed with calm deliberation the surroundings, and finding myself in a dependent position without any rations, or friends to aid, in the enemies' country, and my physical condition very much impaired, an emergency existed that had to be considered with great caution, to avoid recapture. I decided to go directly from the railroad as far into the country during the night as possible, where escaped prisoners would not be expected. I remembered that Lieut. Bowling had directed me to go to Emmetsburg, Md., where I would find the McBride family, true and tried friends to the Southern cause.

I started in a westerly direction taking a star for my guide, traveling an untrodden path through the dark, crossing roads, fields and woods, surrounding all houses, to avoid personal contact. The later grew the night the greater my fatigue, and my wounds, bruised and blistered feet, became very painful. Thus I traveled all night, until just before day; I did not think it safe to travel through that country in the day, and I decided to find a hiding-place where I could rest securely. I could not see myself except through my mental vision and if I should look to others as my feelings indicated; I would be so unlike the natives of that country; I would be taken up as a suspicious character.

This was an old thickly settled country and hiding places were hard to find except in barns of straw, which was also the best protection against the cold weather. The houses were very numerous, and it was difficult to tell a barn from other houses in the dark. I approached a settlement and while prowling around to find the barn, the barking of a dog forbade my approach, and I retired quietly and sought another place. At the next settlement I found a barn, the body of which was made of rough logs, the doors were closed but I climbed up the outer wall and found the back of the barn full of straw. I landed over in the hay and made me a bed deep down in the pile. I was not prepared for the exposure and physical effort the emergency required from train to barn, having languished five months in close confinement on an ice-bound isle in Lake Erie, during which time I was sick, near unto death, of diphtheria from which I had not fully recovered. But amid my afflictions, I felt I had achieved a victory over the enemy, and that satisfied to some extent my patriotic ambition.

Thus reclining in my bed of straw, a deep sleep came upon me and banished all doubts and fears. During my slumber the King of Day lifted the curtains of that eventful night that had covered my successful retreat to this hiding place, and called out the people on the place to their domestic duties, and I was aroused from my slumber by a confusion of tongues which I recognized as the voice of two women talking in an unknown language. They were raking, scraping and stamping over the barn floor, and talking in an angry tone. I listened in breathless silence to catch an intelligible word, but their Dutch language continued with increased fury, as I lay in a very cramped-up position, afraid to move. I supposed someone saw me enter the barn and had come to search for me, and as I had no excuse for occupancy, I decided in case they found me to appear deaf, dumb and crazy, and they speaking Dutch, an explanation would be impossible. But they soon relieved my suspense by leaving the barn, evidently to feed the cattle around the barn.

They soon entered the barn again and commenced pulling hay from the pile in which I was secreted, and as every pull would shake the pile, I felt in eminent danger of slipping down among them; they again left the barn and the old creaking lot gate gave notice of their departure; their voices died away in the distance. I have ever been thankful that I did not snore in my sleep for if I had been snoring when they entered the barn, the result might have been different.

I now assumed a more comfortable position and sweet sleep assumed supremacy over the cares and affliction of the hour; I awoke once more during the day and again after night. Preparatory to another night's adventure I left my bed of straw and crept cautiously down into the barn-yard. It was a dark, cold night and I was lost and bewildered, not knowing what direction to go. After rambling around awhile, I found a public road and decided what course would best suit my purpose.

This was the night of the 12th of February, 1864. The road was frozen, rough, and rocky and at almost every settlement I passed on the road, I had a dog fight; the dogs were all turned loose and they were very numerous. When I retreated they followed and when I made a stand they were satisfied to set in the road and bark at me, and their howling would wake the vigilance of the neighbors' dogs ahead and they challenged my approach as an invading foe. They seemed to recognize me as a Rebel and I concluded that Lee, Jackson or Morgan had passed that way and made an unfavorable impression upon the animal creation in that country, returning from Gettysburg.

Thus passed the early part of that dark, dogged night. Later in the night the dog excitement ceased, and I tramped along unchallenged.

The road was rough and rocky and in addition to other afflictions I suffered greatly from blistered feet, physical exhaustion and hunger. The King of Day began to illume the eastern horizon, and would soon expose me to the criticism of an unfriendly people, but I could not longer wander in darkness or hide during the day in secret places without food. I had already fasted from about 6 o'clock p m. February 11th to 6 a m., February 13th, and had no knowledge of when or how I would get relief. I had been wandering all night in darkness among crossroads and forked roads, through a rough, hilly country; lost and misled from any desired course, I sought rest and retirement in a secluded place beneath the frosty-covered boughs of fallen trees a short distance from the road, where I might recover my physical force, and mature plans for the day's travel.

For the first time since my escape I took a good look at myself and found that my wounds and bruises received at my fall from the train were healing up nicely but I was a little disfigured.

While resting here in seclusion, I resolved upon a bold, aggressive plan of action; I did not know the names of persons, towns, or things by which I might locate my geographical situation and I was not prepared to meet any one or ask any intelligent questions.

Trusting Providence for the result, I came out in the public road and started with all the manly courage that circumstances would warrant, and in a short time I saw a man coming on a white mule, whistling a familiar tune and beating time to his tune with a stick on his old mule. He exhibited a careless, indifferent disposition, just such a man as would best suit my purpose. "Good Morning," said I, "Good Morning" said he. "Please tell me how far it is to (hesitating as if to remember a forgotten name) "Manchester," said he. "Yes," said I, "Manchester, nine miles," said he. To meet a white mule on a cold frosty morning is a sure sign of good luck; here my luck changed and my prospects brightened. Invested with this important information, I felt greatly relieved and determined to go to Manchester, buy me a book as a sample copy, assume the name of Charlie Duncan and travel as a Book-agent, until I could reach my Emmetsburg friends. During my random travel the two previous nights I had wandered across the line of Pennsylvania into Maryland, about 40 miles from my-desired destination.

In addition to other adverse conditions a very cold blizzard blowing with increasing fury from the north, met me before I reached Manchester. In the afternoon I came in sight of the little city. I stopped at an old dilapidated settlement near the road occupied by an old lady and a little boy; age and destitution was noticeably impressed upon this habitation. This good old lady invited me in and made me welcome; it seemed to me that a kind Providence had directed me to this place where I obtained relief and information that I could not have expected in a palace.

Sitting in an old arm-chair by an old fashioned fire-place, an old coffee pot simmering on the embers and dispensing old Rio aroma from its spout, the old lady asked me if I would have a cup of coffee. I accepted with thanks and told her I was very hungry, and would like to have something to eat, and she cheerfully supplied me with such as she had, which was the first food or nourishment I had had from the 11th to the evening of the 13th of February. After resting, warming and lunching, I engaged the old lady in a general conversation, in order to elicit desirable information. She talked very freely and intelligently; I led the conversation to the Civil War and spoke of the suffering soldiers in the field of strife, exposed to the cold, bleak winds that were then blowing intensely. She also expressed herself as being very much opposed to the war. I ascertained the names and political proclivities of several prominent citizens in the town where I expected to sojourn that night.

The greatest antagonism existed between the two political parties—the Radicals for, and the Copperheads against the war.

The extreme cold weather discouraged my progress and traveling as a stranger through a thickly populated country, agitated by political strife; among detectives looking for spies, deserters, and blockade-runners, my successful escape was doubtful and I procured the names of several conservative citizens who would be most likely to help me if necessary.

41

Thus invested with information to meet probable emergencies, I thanked the good lady for courtesies and substantial benefits, and placed in her hand a five dollar gold piece, all the money I had, to pay for my entertainment; she refused pay, and returned the money.

It was now late in the evening of the 13th of February 1864, as I left the humble cabin home, with gratitude overflowing and started to Manchester, to seek refuge from a snow storm that was then raging. I had gone but a short distance when a swift messenger boy from the charitable old lady overtook me and gave me a nice, knit woolen scarf which I have kept sacred to the memory of this humble habitation, (59 years, 1864-1923.)

I entered the city late in the evening, bought a book, (as premeditated), containing a record of the incidents of the war, biographical sketches of Generals, etc., and paid for it out of my five dollar gold piece. I wrapped it up nicely, went to the hotel, registered my name as Charlie Duncan from Baltimore, Md., and represented myself as a Book Agent.

I quietly retired to my room and sought an interview with the landlord who gave me desired information; I inquired the way to Emmetsburg, where I expected to find friends; I learned that Westminster was 9 miles north, and directly on my way to Emmetsburg, and he informed me also that a hack was going to Westminster the next morning. I sent for the young man who was to drive the hack, and made my wishes known to him, and after a friendly talk, he proposed to give me a seat in his buggy to Westminster where I stopped at the hotel and registered as before.

It was now 22 miles to Emmetsburg and I learned the mail hack left for that place the next day at 11 o'clock. I represented to the landlord that I wished to take the next hack to Emmetsburg. On the morning of the 15th the weather continued very severe; the lobby and sitting room of the hotel was crowded and upon entering the room I noticed a Yankee Soldier sitting by the stove, dressed in Federal uniform; I watched him very closely, I saw him speak a few words to an old gentleman and they both at once looked at me in a suspicious manner, which was unmistakable evidence to me that I was the subject of their conversation. I was watching everyone with a critic's eye, feeling sure I had been spotted by the Federal soldier, I did not wait for the mail hack. After paying my hotel bill, I had only 35 cents left, I had no baggage but my book. I told the landlord I would go out in town and return in time to take the hack for Emmetsburg. I took my book and started, walking from street to street, turning corners to avoid spotters. I started toward Emmetsburg, a distance of 22 miles through snow six inches deep, leaving tracks behind me which I could not obliterate.

I was about three hours ahead of the mail hack; I had left my seat vacant which I had engaged, and I feared it would confirm suspicion and start detectives on my trail. I traveled in great suspense during the day, I had gone 15 miles towards Emmetsburg and stopped at a farm-house to warm and rest, where the hack passed me. Late in the evening I continued my journey until the severe weather forced me to seek shelter for the night. To the right of the road stood a fine farm residence with attractive environments, the smoke from the fire flues gushing out above the snow-capped roof, indicating comfort and happiness within. When in contrast with my condition, I was fully prepared to appreciate the feelings and adopt the sentiments of the old, homeless poet, when he was writing "Home Sweet Home." The intervening space between the house and myself was carpeted with snow; the icicles fell and crashed from the limbs along the way. With fears and doubts, as to my reception, I approached the house; my call was answered by a young lady through the door, slightly ajar, who bade me wait until my request could be made known to her father. The father bade me enter and conducted me to a seat in a warm, comfortable room; he made some inquiry about my mode of traveling; I told him I had no conveyance, that I was a passenger on the mail hack and I got so cold, I had to stop and warm, and the hack left me; that I came to see if I could stay at his house tonight. "All right," said he. The room was well furnished and richly decorated with relics rare, arranged in artistic style. I could not realize the extreme condition.

Before and after entering the house, I tried to appear natural and easy. As I sat in a costly cushioned chair, but the congestive reaction of nature seeking to restore its equilibrium, forbade the ease and elegance that might have been reasonably expected of a young gentleman from the city of Baltimore. The effect of the cold blizzard to which I had been exposed, yielded to a normal condition; the farmer had completed his round of domestic duties, and as he entered the room I introduced myself to him as Charlie Duncan from Baltimore. "And my name,, said he "is Bowers."

Supper was announced, and I met Mrs. Bowers and Miss Sallie Bowers at the table. After eating a warm supper and meeting this beautiful young lady, I felt happy and grateful for this unexpected hospitality. I made myself as pleasant and agreeable as possible with the family, and especially with the daughter, whose smiles and pleasant words challenged my admiration, and dissipated the gloom of my eventful struggle for liberty. I wanted to unbosom myself to this good family and tell them all about my troubles and travels, but Mr. Bowers was not in sympathy with the Confederate cause; he was a very strong Union man; his political principles did not agree with mine, and my fictitious name and assumed business were indispensable factors in my effort to escape.

I retired that night with the comfortable assurance of sweet sleep. The next morning was cold and cloudy; I entered the parlor and was greeted by Miss Sallie with smiles and pleasant words. Her fresh lily-white face, the clean white collar around her classic neck were taken for unmistakable evidence of felicitous approbation.

Under such propitious circumstances I felt inclined to remain until the snow clouds rifted, and the weather moderated. It was only 4 miles to Emmetsburg, where I expected to meet my friends, but as they were kept under strict military servility by the Federals, I deemed it best to meet them after night. Therefore, it was necessary to adopt a dilatory programme in order to enter the city after night. My financial condition had become very unhealthy and claimed my serious consideration; I had only 35 cents left and my bill unpaid. Amid the genial cheer of Miss Sallie's smiles and blushes, my financial condition was very embarrassing. Mr. Bowers entered the parlor and referred to the weather, said it was very severe weather to travel; I agreed with him and suggested that if it met his approbation I would remain over until afternoon. He cheerfully

44

invited me to do so, and made me welcome; Miss Sallie was pleased with the arrangement. She had been telling me about a beautiful and accomplished young lady from Baltimore who was visiting a neighbor nearby, and as I was also from Baltimore, it seemed that her greatest desire was to get her two young Baltimore friends together. She described her friend as being a full-fledged Baltimore maiden of 20, flippant in speech and very impulsive; she sent for her friend. Oh, how I wished for a cyclone to come and confuse her plans. I had never been to Baltimore, and did not know any person, place or thing in the city. She came over, we met in the parlor, each, with anticipations unknown to the other.

Being confronted by a Baltimore lady of loquacious tongue and intelligence I could not afford to be interrogated and at once assumed an aggressive manner of speech, and supposing there was a Baltimore street in the city, I asked her if she was acquainted on Baltimore street. She answered in the negative, I felt cheerful over her negative position, and wishing to master the situation more fully, I asked her if she knew several of my friends in the city. She did not know them. I remembered that General Tremble (whom I left a prisoner on Johnson's Island) was from Baltimore, and at the mention of his name she remembered something about him. I told her he was formerly a friend of mine, but since he had dropped over on the Rebel side I had cut his acquaintance.

The war was the all-absorbing topic that day; it was impossible to converse long with any one, without drifting into war events, and intense feeling of sectional strife manifested itself as they spoke of their loved, lost, or suffering ones, who were victims of the cruel war.

Mr. Bowers and family were conservative Union people, but this young lady from Baltimore was quite radical on war questions, and expressed an unfavorable opinion of a young man who would go through the country as a book agent while so many of her friends and relatives were in the war. I defended myself the best I could, and soon changed the subject.

Dinner was announced and disposed of in due form, and we all re-assembled in the parlor. It was now three o'clock p m., February

16th, 1864. The time had come for me to leave or renew my arrangements; my bill was due and unpaid, and I only had 35 cents on hand. The old gentleman had already refused to buy my book, and I proposed to give him a book as a present, and asked him to show it to his neighbors and use his influence in my interest. When I come to deliver I felt sure I could do well. He thanked me very kindly, and when his heart was full of gratitude, I asked my bill. He charged me nothing and invited me to call again. I bid farewell to my friends whom I had deceived so successfully, and entered the war-path again for Emmetsburg, expecting to meet my friends that night.

After a dilatory and cautious march of four or five miles I came in sight of the lamp lights of the city. The nearer I approached the city the brighter grew the lights, and I soon walked the lamp-lit pavements of Emmetsburg in the full anticipation of meeting friends to whom I could reveal my proper name and true condition.

My prospective friend was a merchant; I ascertained his place of business, passed by his door, looked in to see if conditions favored a personal interview with him, and to be sure that he was the man to whom I had been directed. He had been described to me so that I could not mistake his identity; at first sight I was fully satisfied that he was the man I wanted to see; he was behind his counter, busy and alone. I entered and asked, "Is this Mr. McBride?" "Yes sir," said he. I continued, "Well sir, you are the man I want to see, you have been recommended to me as an honorable and confidential gentleman, and as such I would like to have a private talk with you." Mr. McBride locked his front door and conducted me to the back room of his store. Shivering with cold, I seated myself in a warm, cozy room, face to face with a venerable fatherly old gentleman, to whom I introduced myself as R. D. Chapman, Captain Company E, 55th Georgia Regiment, C. S. A., an escaped prisoner, and as a further evidence of my true identity I told him that Lieut. Bowling who was wounded and captured at Gettysburg, gave me the name of your daughter, Miss Annie McBride, and requested me to call on you.

46

This statement satisfied Mr. McBride that I was not a detective trying to criminate him, and with manifestations of tender compassion he assured me that I was as safe with him as in my own father's home.

He administered such comforts and refreshments as was best adapted to my temporary relief; he excused himself for a short time and left me seated by a warm stove. Quite a radical change had been experienced; the bright light in the warm comfortable room had superseded the dark cold night of doubt and fear, and as a storm-riven vessel, I had entered a port of safety.

As I sat brooding over these happy results, Mr. McBride entered the room followed by five tall, fine looking gentlemen. At this silent approach from a dark alley through a back door, I thought I had been betrayed. Mr. McBride seeing my excitement, said, "Fear not, these are your friends," which was corroborated by their friendly grip, kind words, and approving smiles. After many words of cheer and best wishes each of them gave me some pocket change and departed, leaving my old friend and me to ourselves.

His family had been advised of my coming. He conducted me through a dark alley to the rear entrance of his residence; the door stood ajar to receive the escaped prisoner, and I was cautiously ushered into the presence of the family and introduced to the wife and two daughters of Mr. McBride. They bade me be seated in the vacant chair of their affectionate son and brother who a year before had left this loving group to take part in the Southern army.

For the first time since my capture I sat in the midst of sympathizing friends. The doors and windows were well secured against enemies and eavesdroppers, while I related briefly the eventful struggle through which I had passed; and as I proceeded they nestled closely around the table and listened to my story with mingled tears of sympathy and smiles of joy, known only to grief stricken parents who had given their sons to the cause of liberty. This family had passed through the reign of terror and oppression when "Maryland, My Maryland" was penned by the poet, and sung by the patriots.

This once happy home had been invaded by its political enemies, who arrested and imprisoned the father for the expression of Southern sympathy, and forced the son to seek refuge in the Southern army, leaving the defenseless family alone amid revolutionary strife; and all these troubles seemed to be fresh in their minds and struggling for utterance without adequate words of expression.

This home was known to be friendly to the Confederate cause and a refuge for the unfortunate, belligerent, and the house was often raided by the Federate, and for fear of a surprise that night the old gentleman conducted me to a safe place of hiding, should they be disturbed.

I then retired and slept soundly during the night. The morning of the 17th was bright and clear; the warm bed, cozy room, kind welcome, and Christian sympathy which I enjoyed, suggested a day of thanksgiving, and my glad heart rejoiced all day, over the cheerful hope of a successful escape.

Next in order was the family greeting, a warm breakfast, followed by parlor entertainments. This family consisted of father, mother, two daughters and a son in the Southern Maryland Line.

Miss Annie McBride was my constant companion during the day and at intervals her mother and sister contributed their smiles and cheerful words to render my sojourn pleasant. General Lee's march to Gettysburg and events connected with the campaign were fresh in the minds of Miss McBride and with the devotion of a Roman Catholic woman, true to her convictions, she loved the Confederate cause and honored Confederate soldiers. Among her many soldier friends, she referred very tenderly to Lieut. Bowling of Mississippi, whom she met in the hospital at Gettysburg. She revealed to him her sympathy for him and his cause; fortunately for me, Lieut. Bowling was in prison with me and communicated to me such information as directed me to this good lady's home.

While the family entertained me during the day, the father was not idle. He learned that John Akin of Baltimore (a member of the Southern Maryland Line) was on furlough in the Federal lines visiting friends and relatives. John was in the vicinity of Emmetsburg on his return to the Southern Army. Mr. McBride ascertained the whereabouts of John Akin, and informed him that he had a Confederate Captain in his care who desired to be guided through to the Confederate lines. John cheerfully accepted the task, and the preliminaries were arranged for our meeting. John Akin assumed a fictitious name and was dressed in disguise; the Akin name was too well-known in Baltimore and throughout Maryland. Dr. Akin, John's father was Professor of Chemistry in the Maryland Institute, at Baltimore; therefore John Akin changed his name to John Dee, and dressed in a citizens' suit with white scarf around his neck by which I was to know him, and it was understood that he was to know me by having on Mr. McBride's overcoat; it was further agreed that John and I should meet six miles from Emmetsburg on the road to Fredericksburg.

Mr. McBride returned that evening and informed me of his arrangements, and hasty preparations were made to join John at the appointed time and place. They gave me a small valise and a few articles of necessary clothing. The old gentleman gave me his overcoat, and to avoid suspicion he ordered the mail coach to call for a gentleman passenger at the Catholic boarding house at 4 a m. Mr. McBride gave me a note of only three words to the proprietor of the boarding house, saying "Entertain the Stranger." I left this good family with their blessings and prayers that I might reach my home in safety.

I was directed to a large Cathedral in the rural part of the city: I delivered my note to the proprietor who bade me enter and be welcome. I registered my original fictitious name and assumed my book agency. After a good night's sleep and a 4 o'clock breakfast, all the passengers were ready and waiting for the coach. The white scarf, the overcoat, the six mile stranger to be recognized as my traveling companion—all rendered the 18th day of February, 1864 a day of suspense and anticipation.

I arrived at the six mile village about 8 o'clock, looking with all my eyes for John Dee who was to guide me through the Federal lines and across the Potomac river into the Confederate lines.

As the coach rolled up to the stopping place, I saw my man as described; I stepped out of the coach, I looked at him and he at me; we recognized each other at first sight but did not speak. We secured seats together in the coach, old Father McBride's old seamless overcoat was too large for me, and John criticised the fit of my overcoat and I criticised the style of the white scarf around his neck.

On we went with a good speed and arrived at Fredrick's City at one o'clock. We secured a room at the hotel and went into secret session for an hour and arranged plans for our future progress. I knew nothing about the country or people and had but little advice to offer except caution and safety. I committed myself to the care and conduct of my new friend, John Dee; I recognized in him a bold, daring adventurer of a very aggressive style, and of a reckless character. My natural characteristics all differed from his, except in our devotion to the common cause. I did not have great confidence in the aggressive policy of my new conductor, especially now, when we were so near the Federal lines, where spies and detectives were lurking around every public place looking for deserters and Blockade Runners. We started about 4 o'clock p m. toward the Potomac river, 13 miles south; John Dee had entered the Federal lines the third time to visit his friends and relatives in Baltimore; he was well acquainted with the country and had friends ahead where he expected to stop and get information as to the position of the Federal Pickets along the Potomac river. We reached the first friend 4 miles from the Potomac about dark, where we were told a large picket force had been stationed along the river and that we would be in imminent danger of being captured should we attempt to cross. Worn down with fatigue and discouragement I favored returning to the interior and looking for a less perilous way of escape, but my invincible young leader urged me to go on two miles further towards the Potomac, where we expected more reliable tidings. We ventured on in the dark to the second friend who told us we were very near the picket zone of the Potomac, and advised us to retreat under cover of the night to a place of safety; we rested with this friend a portion of the night and returned to Fredrick City, where we held another council of war and agreed to disagree and each one to go alone.

My plan was to go slow and cautious, avoid all danger points, leave the country and small towns, and abide in the city of Baltimore until I could find an unguarded point in the Federal lines.

This plan did not suit my friend, John Dee; he had been visiting relatives and friends in Baltimore and vicinity for several weeks, and under the circumstances he could not return to the city, but he thought it would be a very safe place for me. He gave me a letter of introduction to his father in Baltimore, and wishing each other a safe return to Dixie, I took the first train for the city of Baltimore, and arrived there February 20th, 1864.

I stopped at a hotel and registered as Henry R. Jackson from Ohio, ostensibly a Medical Student desiring to matriculate. On the 21st, I called on Dr. Akin the Professor of Chemistry in the Maryland Institute; I found him alone in his department and presented my letter of introduction from his son John, giving my proper name and rank. He read the note, looked at me and read the note again, and asked me about his son John. I told him how, when and where I met John; that we failed to cross the Potomac river and returned to the interior; I told him of my capture and escape, and asked for such aid and assistance as would facilitate my journey home. I found him to be a grand, old, patriotic American nobleman, of the true, Maryland type; he told me he was not able to do anything for me, but he would introduce me to a union man who could assist me, and requested me to call again that evening at twilight. Accordingly, I did so. He had advised some of his benevolent friends of my presence, and said the good ladies would assist me the next day; he then conducted me through back alleys into a large hat house and introduced me to Mr. Harry Nicely and placed me in his hands for safe-keeping with the request that I call again. Harry Nicely was a liberal, free-spoken man of noble characteristics; he informed me that I looked too much like a Rebel, and he proposed to reconstruct me. I told him to proceed with his reconstruction process. He invested me with a nice, new suit of clothes, hat, shirt, shoes and all; took me into a barber shop as a country friend and ordered the barber to shave, shear, and shampoo me preparatory to matriculation in a medical college. Thus transformed, Harry and I parted to meet at 9 o'clock next day.

I called on my friends at the appointed time and enjoyed with them the celebration of General Washington's birthday the 22nd of February, 1864, and my grateful heart was filled to overflowing when Dr. Akin handed me a package containing $103.00 presented by the ladies of Baltimore to the unseen and unknown Captain of Co. E, 55th Georgia Regiment, C. S. A. The length of time, and the ruthlessness of conquest has never abated my gratitude to these kind and generous friends of Baltimore and Emmetsburg, who aided me in my time of trouble and distress, and made escape possible.

Harry Nicely, one of my most gracious friends, had formerly lived in the Valley of Virginia, near the Baltimore and Ohio Railroad and he was well acquainted with the geography of the country occupied by the Federals, through which I would have to pass. He advised me to take the Baltimore and Ohio train from Baltimore and after passing Harper's Ferry, leave the train at Duffield Station or Kerneysville and travel south.

He gave me the name of Mr. McIntire near Duffield Station, and the names of other friends in the Virginia valley who were known to the Federals as Union men, but to them the mention of his name, would be my passport and a guarantee of a hearty welcome to me. Thus my plan of travel made, and instructions given, and being well clad, shod, shaved and sheared, invested with money, reinforced, by 5 days feasting in Baltimore, I assumed the name of Mr. R. A. Clayton and resumed my Book Agency.

I left Baltimore on the night train with the intention of stopping off at Duffield Station as advised by my friend Nicely, but the night train was a through train, and did not stop at any small towns or stations, therefore I had to stop at Harper's Ferry, or go on to Wheeling; and Wheeling being entirely out of my line of travel, I stopped at Harper's Ferry, Va., late in the night of the 26th of February, 1864.

With many other passengers I marched under a strong guard to the Provost Headquarters, where each passenger had to sign his name, from what place, going to what place, and on what business. In a large record book, I signed, R. A. Clayton, from Baltimore, going to Wheeling, Book Agent. We were then released and directed to the hotel; I found the hotel crowded with Federal officers and soldiers, the benches, tables and floor in the hotel were all occupied by the sleeping, snoring patriots.

The day dawned, breakfast was served, the Federate dispersed; I commenced looking for a way of escape from Harper's Ferry; I failed to find any possible way of escape; I applied to the Provost Marshal for a permit to go on to Wheeling, but was informed that transient travel was forbidden on the railroad from Harper's Ferry, and I gave up in despair. Walled in by huge mountains on every side, in the forks of two rivers, the Potomac on the north, the Shenandoah on the south and the precipitous cliffs of Shenandoah heights intervening. The bridge across the Potomac and the roads between the rivers and the rock-ribbed heights were all strongly guarded. Two brigades of Federal soldiers were encamped on the summit of the heights; my escape by day was absolutely impossible and I sought retirement and needful rest in my room during the day, preparatory to making a desperate effort to escape at night.

Late in the evening I walked out to the foot of the mountain and joined a company of playful boys, jumping, skipping and throwing rocks into the river, etc. Being the oldest boy in the company and having an object in view, I soon became a leading character among the boys, and at my request we all ascended the stone steps to the large old cemetery on the peak of Shenandoah Heights, overlooking the country in every direction; and while the boys were busy showing me the tombs of the distinguished dead, I made a careful survey of the Federal Camps on the summit of the mountain, which extended from brink to brink; and as far as I could see the white tents covered the mountain top, and the rugged precipitous slope of the mountain between the camp guard and the pickets at the foot of the mountain, was the only un-guarded way of escape, and that was a perilous adventure involving doubt and danger. The stone wall enclosing the cemetery was 4 feet high, and we could be seen over the wall by the soldiers as they passed by, but when night approached the boys left me alone, and I sought a hiding place among the tombs until dark.

Sitting in the city of the dead on Shenandoah Heights, a lofty mountain peak pointing to, and overlooking the junction of the Shenandoah and the Potomac rivers, I viewed with mingled sadness and admiration the magnificent grandeur of Maryland Heights beyond the Potomac, and as twilight was falling upon the vision that so challenged my admiration, music bands of the different regiments, commenced playing martial music, which was grand, as it echoed and re-echoed among the mountain cliffs and down the rushing rivers. But their martial music in those days was not in unison with the sonorous chords in the heart of a Confederate soldier; and as they played "Yankee, Doodle," my sad, silent soul responded, "Dixie."

The bands ceased playing, Tat-too sounded and silence succeeded all, except the dashing rivers and rushing wind.

Starting and stumbling over the graves of departed spirits, a superstitious imagination unbidden arose and in my human weakness through mental vision I could see the spirits of Federal soldiers and John Brown's fanatics waiting to forbid my going. But reinforced by the thought that Stonewall Jackson's heroes and other Confederate dead from victorious Battlefields were also there, in a spiritual sense I was not alone. The great Captain who never lost a battle was with me and bid me go and fear no evil.

With a resolution equal to the emergency I mounted the stone wall and by the aid of the camp fires I soon located the picket line. Carefully avoiding the Pickets I made my way to the brink of the mountain; planting my foot upon a firm foundation and holding fast to the bushes, I cautiously descended the mountain slope so as to pass out between the Camp Guard on the summit and the Pickets at the foot of the mountain. I surveyed during the day this mountain the best I could, to ascertain the possibility of my escape. From the river up the Shenandoah slope presented the appearance of irregular wall of rock, precipices, cliffs and caverns, partially covered with bushes growing among the rocks, and I was fully aware of the perilous adventure; I proceeded slowly walking and crawling, feeling my way with feet and hands to avoid danger points. Thus I passed two Brigades of Federal Camps and I felt that I had left Harper's

Ferry by a route that had never been traveled by man. This new route diverted me from my original instructions and I therefore changed my direction toward the Baltimore and Ohio railroad and proceeded as directed by my Baltimore friends. At a late hour while passing Duffield Station I was halted by the guard posted in the road near the station, he called the sergeant of the guard, who came and inquired into my business. I represented to him that I was a citizen living in that vicinity, had been out nursing a sick neighbor and was on my way home, and upon these reasonable representations he released me, for which I thanked him kindly and invited him to come out and dine with me the next day, which invitation he very graciously accepted and expressed a desire to become acquainted with some of the citizens in the country during his stay in camp at Duffield station. He had no orders to detain the citizens but had strict orders to arrest all soldiers and deserters without proper leave of absence. After a pleasant talk around the camp fire, one of the guards walked with me across the picket line and bid me a happy good night on my way, and it was certainly a happy good night for me, far more successful than I could have reasonably anticipated. This night was the critical period in my struggle for the priceless liberty or a loathsome prison. I had now passed all the danger points and felt that I had made the supreme sacrifice during the night of February 26th, 1864, to the full limit of human endurance.

The day of the 27th was now dawning and two miles yet to go before reaching the home of my first Southern sympathizer in the Virginia valley; he received me very cautiously and did not introduce me into the social circle of his family until I told him that I had a message to him from our mutual friend, Mr. Harry Nicely of Baltimore, Md., who requested me to call on him to whom I could reveal my troubles and desires with safety. After relating briefly my capture, escape and present condition I found that Harry Nicely's name was an acceptable passport to the home and the hearts of this worthy sympathetic family. Harry Nicely formerly lived in the Virginia valley and was favorably known for his generous hospitality which characterized the citizenship of Virginia valley during the war.

A large portion of the Virginia valley was dominated by the Federal forces subject to lawless raiding parties who invaded the homes of the Southern sympathizers and carried all the men away to prison; therefore all the men who remained at home and the soldiers on furlough had secret hiding places, and the ladies of the home were always on the lookout for approaching strangers whom they regarded as enemies until they were fully identified and their business made known. I soon established my identity as R. D. Chapman, Captain of Company E, 55th Georgia Regiment, Confederate States Army and enjoyed the confidence and kind hospitality of this patriotic sympathetic family during the day.

The two sleepless nights and the rough experience of the last night tested my physical strength and endurance to its limit; this day was the Sabbath day, and for one time in my life I obeyed the Lord's commandments and kept His day Holy, after the very needful bathing, feasting, resting and sleeping. I was much better prepared to continue my journey south.

The comfort and kind hospitality of this distinguished family, their patriotic sympathy and expressions of joy for my successful escape thus far, their cordial good will and wishes for my future success reversed by condition in one days' time from distress and mental agony to the realization of a grateful friendship and aid that inspires a hope of my future success. Thus equipped for my journey south I felt that I could safely proceed. I traveled only during the night as directed by my Baltimore friend, Harry Nicely.

Early in the night of February 27th I bade the family an affectionate farewell; the father walked with me a mile or two through fields, forest and farm gates, avoiding public roads and high-ways where Federal vidette were posted and where the lawless war tramps, gamblers, robbers and bandits perpetrated their atrocious deeds.

Traveling as directed by my first friend three miles south, I arrived at the place of my second friend at about the midnight hour; after calling several times, a lady from an upper window answered my call. I delivered the message from their Baltimore friend and was admitted and made very welcome by the good lady of the house. The husband was absent and did not come in until I had been fully identified to the satisfaction of the wife; he appeared as a courtly, cultured gentleman and she as an elegant type of Virginia womanhood. For two hours I rested in a warm cozy room feasting on cake and wine, as I revealed to them a brief sketch of my capture and escape. On my departure the lady urged me to partake freely of the wine and the husband proposed a patriotic toast to the heroes of the South. I responded to their toast with expressions of gratitude for their kindness to me during my sojourn with them.

My third friend lived four miles south on the pike, a public highway very much traveled by the enemy and others unfriendly to the south. This distance had to be covered during the night; every hour of the day was unsafe for the stranger on the highway who could not identify himself as a citizen or a soldier with proper authority.

One mile of this distance was to be traveled on the pike, a very public high-way; this mile was quickly made under the exhilarating influence of the wine administered to me at the last station which bid defiance to the rough, cold, dark night and landed me safe at the gate of my third friend before day dawn of the 28th of February, 1864, where I expected to rest during the day. Here I was also admitted, and received the sympathetic hospitality characteristic of the Virginia valley farmer. I explained my condition as briefly as possible and promised to explain to him more fully during the day, after needful rest and sleep. I was invited to dinner where I met the family who were glad to see me and hear my war experience. This was a large interesting family of boys and girls who listened to my story with great interest. They also had a war story to tell, little Johnnie broke in and said: "Oh! Papa tell him about the Rebel camp." "Yes" said the father, "we have a Rebel camp on the mountain two miles from here; five or six of the Virginia Cavalry are here on furlough visiting their relatives and friends; they have located a camp in the thicket on the mountain where they keep their horses; they will start south tonight to rejoin their commands; they have an extra horse to carry out with them."

This was good news for me and he proposed to get a saddle and arrange for me to ride south with the cavalry boys. All things were made ready to start south early in the night; we all assembled at the Rebel camp where we met the grief-stricken relatives, sweethearts and friends who indulged freely in crying, kissing and affectionate fare-well words as we mounted our horses and started down through the dark, dense forest, carefully avoiding the Federal picket post on the pike road a few miles south. I was very proud of my military escort; they were trained Virginia cavaliers, all well-armed, brave, fearless soldiers; our leader was a practical army scout and knew every country path and private trail between the Blue Ridge mountains and the military highways in the Virginia valley. He soon led us into the Rebel path known and used only by the Confederate soldiers, scouts, and spies for their ingress and egress from the lower to the upper Virginia valley region.

We had about ninety miles to travel before entering the Confederate lines. This route led us through woods, fields and thirty farm gates during the night; the speed of our horses was so regulated as to make thirty miles before daylight. The early part of the night was dark, the road rough and muddy, the cold winter wind was extremely disagreeable to me. I could see my way but dimly and often fell behind, but by urging my horse I kept near the company, our heroic leader riding the fleetest horse in advance within hailing distance giving signals when necessary to speed up or slow down. The speed-up order came too often for me; I was on the slowest and the poorest horse in the company and in rear guard service all night. Later in the night the cheerful moonlight began to illuminate our path-way and during the remainder of the night we had a bright moonlight view of the fields, forest and natural scenery through which we passed. Having passed from darkness into a delightful moonlight night was certainly a great relief and pleasure to our company, but it did not mitigate my suffering condition; this was my third night's travel without sleep and unaccustomed to horse-back riding, I was suffering with pain and physical exhaustion and no relief except the exercise of heroic endurance. It was this characteristic endurance that was ever present with me through all the disadvantages and hardships of a Confederate soldier in active service during the Civil War that comforted me through severe illness in a loathsome prison, and inspired a living hope of my successful escape that grew brighter as we approached the Confederate line.

Riding briskly all night we passed the thirty mile station on the Rebel path at the dawn of day, February 29th, 1864, where we camped around a warm fire, fed and rested our horses, and held a council of war; our leader informed us that we had passed the last military post in the Virginia valley and the only danger that we could anticipate during the day was the lawless army of bandits, robbers and gamblers on the public high-way in the neutral zone between the Northern and Southern armies. We unanimously resolved to assume the offensive, raise the black flag and defy any opposition that might intervene between us and the confederate line. To avoid lawless characters on the public high-ways we continued our journey on the Rebel path until late in the evening of February 29th, 1864, when our trail intersected the public highway at a point five miles from the out-post of our Confederate army; these five miles were made in quick time. Here we were halted a short time, and after satisfactory identification we passed the out-post and entered the Confederate lines, March the first, 1864.

Thanking my military escort for their kind protection through the danger zone to a place of safety, I secured conveyance to Staunton, Va., and reported to the hospital for a few days' rest and medical treatment. I then went to Richmond, Va., and applied for identification papers. General Winder referred me to the war office where I found the records of the 55th Georgia Regiment showing that I was Captain of Company E, 55th Georgia Regiment, C. S. A. I obtained an identification certificate and a furlough of thirty days.

The news of my escape had preceded me and was received with great rejoicing among my relatives and friends; at the expiration of my leave of absence I reported to Lieut. Col. Persons, Commander of the Post at Andersonville Prison and was appointed Adjutant of the Post. Here I found a remnant of my regiment who were not captured; they were organized with remnants of other companies into detachments of three companies and known as the 55th Georgia detachment, on duty as prison guards at Andersonville, Ga.

I served as Adjutant at post headquarters from the 15th of June, 1864 to October 15th. During this time the prisoners increased from fourteen thousand to thirty-two thousand, and the capacity of the prison space was increased to thirty acres. Other extensive improvements were planned, but public policy demanded that a large portion of the prisoners should be removed from Andersonville to better and more healthful localities, which superseded the necessity of further improvements, and the transportation of prisoners commenced about the 18th of October, 1864. I assumed command of the Detachment of the 55th Georgia as a prison guard and transported one thousand prisoners to Florence South Carolina, where orders awaited me to report to General Joseph E. Johnson at Savannah, Ga., with my detachment of one hundred and thirty men.

In obedience to this order we were transported by rail to the nearest point to Savanah where we derailed and continued under a forced march over a temporary military road through the rough rice fields of South Carolina; we entered the city in the evening of the 5th day of December, 1864. I reported immediately to General Hardee's Headquarters where I was informed that the city was in great peril and that my command was greatly needed at the front. Without food or rest we were ordered to report to General Mercer's Headquarters, on Lau-ton's farm seven miles west of Savanah; arriving late in the evening, great excitement prevailed at General Mercer's Headquarters. The flood gates of the extensive rice fields around Savannah had been opened. The advance of General Sherman's army had made its appearance in our front, but the flooded area rendered their direct attack upon the city impracticable.

For several miles around the city, cross-ways were constructed over the flooded fields at convenient distances for travel and trade between the country and city. The enemy attempted to enter the city over these cross-ways, but they were repulsed by our artillery and met with such resistance in our front that they sought a bloodless entry into the city through a secret conspiracy with some of the disloyal troops in our camp. An Irish battalion composed of seven full companies of Irishmen known as the galvanized rebels who were supporting our guns entered into a conspiracy led by the orderly sergeants of the seven companies in a general mutiny to be executed at a late hour of the night; they had planned to spike the guns, desert their post and march in a body over the cross-way to the enemies camp, but we had some loyal soldiers, true to the Southern cause in this Irish camp who reported in full their designs to the General's Headquarters; this information was transmitted to me immediately with orders to disarm the Irish battalion and place them under guard for an investigation.

I had just arrived at General Mercer's headquarters at 5 p m., with 130 of my old soldiers and had located my headquarters for the night, after a forced march all day. We were not prepared for any service, but this order was imperative and demanded prompt execution. I ordered my men into line and made ready for action, loaded guns, fixed bayonets and proceeded to the Irish battalion camp, seized their guns and posted a guard around their camp and sent a dispatch to General Mercer's headquarters informing him that his order had been obeyed.

General Mercer and his staff and other officials hastened to the Irish camp, and after a thorough investigation they found that the situation was more serious than was anticipated, the mutinous uprising that was planned to start at I a m. that night included the murder or kidnapping of all of their commissioned officers and all others who resisted. A Court Martial was organized and the orderly Sergeants from each of the seven companies were tried by the court and found guilty of Treason and mutiny, for which they were sentenced to be shot at 2 a m. that night, and the other men of the battalion were carried away under guard. This conspiracy, instigated and planned by our enemies in the Irish battalion, proved to be a signal failure. The timely apprehension and prompt action of our authorities defeated their nefarious scheme and the Confederates still commanded this post.

Withdrawing from our front the invading army sought another point of ingress where they gathered a force on our right flank and advanced on our position through a dense thicket of undergrowth, firing volley after volley as they advanced cautiously upon our picket line through the darkness of the night. As officer of the guard, I had orders to relieve the picket line, evacuate this post at 11 p m. and make a hasty retreat into the city, the enemy advancing nearer and nearer, firing indiscriminately upon our line, and at 11 p m., the minnie balls playing with the forest trees around us gave me notice that quick action was necessary and according to my orders I hastened to my first guard post and found that the guard on post No. I had fled to parts unknown, the second post was also deserted, at the 3rd post I found one of my old true and tried soldiers steady at his post as the boy that stood on the burning deck whence all but him had fled.

Having withdrawn the picket line we made the seven miles into the city in quick time, the pontoon bridge across the Savannah river awaited our arrival in the city and we crossed over the river and continued our march through South Carolina, subject to the orders of General Joseph E. Johnson, in his campaign of defense against the invasion of General Sherman's army.

General Sherman occupied the city of Savanah, where he remained resting and recruiting his army until the 1st of January, 1865, when he continued his march of invasion up the Atlantic coast through South and North Carolina, General Joseph E. Johnson in command of the Confederate forces limited in men and resources, gallantly defended the country against invading parties from Sherman's army.

This was a campaign of great activities, daily fighting, skirmishing and marching through extreme hardships and privations for three months, from the 1st of January, 1865, to Bentonville, North Carolina, where the last and final battles were fought on the 19th, 20th and 21st of March, 1865, after which a peace conference was arranged which culminated in the surrender and in general terms of peace between the Southern and Northern armies. And when our worthy leaders found that resistance was no longer possible, they advised their faithful soldiers to return to their respective places of abode, rebuild their burned and deserted homes, and make as good and faithful citizens as they had been true and faithful soldiers in the service of their country.

The vanquished host of the Confederate soldiers in their destitution, with sadness, turned their backs upon the new made graves of their companions who fell upon the battlefield. Facing homeward and encouraged by the prospects of peace, they raised the banner of Christian civilization as the birthright of American citizenship, and the cherished hope of meeting the loved ones who awaited their coming made their burden light and their cross easy to bear, and when in the full realization of joining hearts and hands with those at home who endured the stress and strain of the Civil war, they wrought mightily together in domestic labor of love in the constructive development of an empire as fruitful and fragrant as the mind could conceive or the hand of man could construct. Characteristic of the trained soldier, ready to battle for victory, they entered into learned professions of law, physic, theology, mechanism and agriculture and in the scientific research they laid bare the vast fields of ocean, earth and air and made ready for the mighty men of inventive genius to touch the electric button that moves the great car of destiny laden with the rich products of commerce, wrought out by the industrial hand of the American citizen.

To the Dear and Noble War Mothers

With a passion of love and sympathy I would cherish the sacred memory of the WAR MOTHERS who passed through the conclusive ordeal of maternity with her soldier boy in her arms whom she has cared for from the cradle to his noble, young man-hood, and when called to the colors of his country, she gives him the last mother's kiss and bids him go and return in honor or never return. Many returned in honor, many did not return, and many returned, only to drop a tear and place a wreath of flowers upon his mother's grave. When in the memory of man, did ere such love and sorrow meet, or thorns compose so rich a crown as bedecked the brow of mother-hood who made this supreme sacrifice. Poets have penned and Bards have sung of the mother's sacred love, but the half has never yet been told.

63

Achievements of a Reunited Nation

The wonderful achievements in constructive development and material progress throughout the American government since the Civil War have obliterated the lines of sectional strife, and there is now no north, no south, no east, no West.

The north has moved south, the east has moved west, and we all live together as friends, neighbors and citizens, under the protection of a re-united nation composed of a sisterhood of states governed by the time honored principals of local self-government and political equality.

A large and worthy citizenship from the north with their capital and labor, their industry and economy, have greatly aided us in building our cities, churches, schools, and in helping us to make the old south new. They have come, married and given in marriage, here among our southern people and the Lord only knows what will be the final result. But whatever fate my come to them, we welcome them and bid them God speed in all of their laudable enterprises, and we congratulate them for the worthy father-hood of a noble, patriotic son-ship who fought shoulder to shoulder with the sons of Confederate Veterans in the World War to make America safe for Democracy, Peace and Humanity, and we extend greetings to all Veterans of the Civil War, who can truly say, I have fought a good fight, I have kept the faith, and when in the full realization of the sacred promises to the faithful and true, we can rest together in peace from our labors and leave a rich legacy to our descendants, with the cherished hope that American Constitutional Liberty will yet have defenders who live free or die.

DEDICATION

As a native son of the South I point with pride to the valor and heroism of the Southern soldiers who have stood in the front rank of every American army, and I am sure that the Sons of Confederate Veterans will perform their part in war or in peace.

Therefore: With a grateful recognition of the Sons of Confederate Veterans, and the United Daughters of the Confederacy, as the proper custodians of Confederate History, and in consideration of their faithful care, beneficent deeds, patriotic devotion to the comfort and pleasure of the Confederate Veterans,

I, hereby dedicate this, by Memorandum and Reminiscences of my War History to the descendants and friends of Confederate Veterans.

(Signed) R. D. CHAPMAN, Capt. Co., E, 55th Georgia Regiment.

March 1, 1923.

THE END

Made in the USA
Middletown, DE
24 September 2023

39168924R00043